THE FLYERS

Susan Catherine Koerner Wright

Bishop Milton Wright

Katharine Wright

Wilbur Wright

Orville Wright

THE FLYERS

IN SEARCH OF WILBUR AND ORVILLE WRIGHT

NOAH ADAMS

THREE RIVERS PRESS • NEW YORK

Published by Three Rivers Press, New York, New York.
Member of the Crown Publishing Group, a division of Random House, Inc.
www.crownpublishing.com

Three Rivers Press and the Tugboat design are registered trademarks of Random House, Inc.

Originally published in hardcover by Crown Publishers, a division of Random House, Inc., in 2003.

Printed in the United States of America

Design by Leonard Henderson

Library of Congress Cataloging-in-Publication Data
Adams, Noah.
The flyers : in search of Wilbur and Orville Wright / by Noah Adams.
1. Wright, Wilbur, 1867–1912.   2. Wright, Orville, 1871–1948.
3. Aeronautics—History.   4. Aeronautics—United States—Biography.   I. Title.
TL540.W7A64   2003
629.13'0092'273—dc22   2003015011

ISBN 0-609-81032-4
10 9 8 7 6 5 4 3 2 1
First Paperback Edition

For
Master Sergeant Randy Crowder, USAF (Ret.)

CONTENTS

PREFACE
xi

CHAPTER ONE
WOODLAND CEMETERY
1

CHAPTER TWO
TO KITTY HAWK
19

CHAPTER THREE
PILOTS AND PLANES
41

CHAPTER FOUR
HUFFMAN PRAIRIE
59

CHAPTER FIVE
ABOVE FRANCE
75

CHAPTER SIX
FORT MYER
93

CONTENTS

CHAPTER SEVEN
NEW YORK HARBOR
115

CHAPTER EIGHT
THE OSHKOSH AIR SHOW
133

CHAPTER NINE
HAWTHORN HILL
157

CHAPTER TEN
FIRST FLIGHT
181

AUTHOR'S NOTE
203

BIBLIOGRAPHY
207

CREDITS
211

INDEX
215

PREFACE

I T TAKES ONLY NINETEEN SECONDS TO WALK THE DISTANCE OF the first flight. But when I was there the wind was up and cold on my face, and I felt as if I'd *entered* the black-and-white photograph I'd been seeing all my life. The sand is light gray, there's a spill of surf in the distance. Wilbur, running at the right of the plane, and Orville, the pilot, are in dark suits. The propellers blur against the sky as the machine rises.

Orville's flight at Kitty Hawk—taking off from level ground into a stiff wind—was the first ever to be controlled and powered. It lasted twelve seconds and covered only 120 feet. Then Wilbur tried, with slight improvement. Orville's next turn added twenty-five feet. Finally, Wilbur took off and held the airplane in a straight line and at almost level altitude for fifty-nine seconds and 852 feet. Two men, somehow, had built a plane with a motor and brought it here from Ohio and flown it almost three times the length of a football field.

✦   ✦

My first trip to North Carolina's Outer Banks was in early November 2001. It was a vacation; I wanted to be at the edge of the Atlantic, to read and listen to the waves, hoping for a storm. Four days passed before I thought to visit the Wright Brothers National Memorial.

Two wooden buildings have been re-created, with the guidance of several old photographs. One was a hangar for the 1903 airplane—the fit was sideways. The other was a workshop, with a kitchen and sleeping space. Not far beyond is the December 17 flight path, marked by a granite boulder at the beginning, and smaller stones at the landing spots, out along a line to the northeast, toward the ocean.

I joined a group of other visitors, listening to a park ranger tell the story of the Wrights and their four trips to Kitty Hawk—by train, I learned, all the way from Dayton to Elizabeth City, North Carolina, and on from there by boat. That's when I first thought I might write about their travels and their flying, because my own great-grandfather managed to find his way into my imagining of the story.

Haskell Wellman, when I was growing up, was a nocturnal old man who kept a workshop and his bed in a back room of our house in Ashland, Kentucky—sometimes I'd hear a quavering song from his violin.

When he was young, Haskell helped start the town's first telephone company, and later opened an electric car dealership. He was known as an inveterate, unschooled inventor. He loved trains, and often visited the depot a few blocks from our house. The Chesapeake & Ohio timetables for the years when the Wrights made their trips to North Carolina indeed show a brief stop in Ashland, and—in my fantasy—it pleases me to think of Wilbur and Orville stepping off the train for the newspapers and some fresh air, and finding themselves in a conversation with Haskell Wellman, thirty-four years old in 1900. The Wrights would have sensed a lively kindred spirit, and might have said, "Why don't you come with us—we're off to the coast to fly airplanes." But, as the 1900 census data shows, Haskell Wellman was a homeowner, eleven years married, with a wife named Damie, her mother, and a four-year-old son named Noah, and perhaps he'd best stay in town.

The Wrights, by contrast, were splendidly unencumbered. Neither had married, they hadn't left home, and had been moderately successful with their own businesses. At the time of the first flight, Wilbur Wright was thirty-six years old, his brother Orville thirty-two. They'd passed up college, becoming printers, then bicycle makers. Their sister, Katharine, was twenty-nine, also single; she'd graduated from Oberlin College and was teaching high school. Milton Wright, their seventy-four-year-old father, was a bishop of the United Brethren Church. The Wrights lived together in a frame house at 7 Hawthorn Street on the West Side of Dayton, Ohio.

For previous books, and in radio work, I've always wanted to go where the story happened, to walk around, talk with people, make notes about what I found most interesting. The story of the Wright Brothers—wonderfully told in several comprehensive biographies—beckons with travel ideas. What was it like on a boat out on the Albemarle Sound when Wilbur first came across? Was their flying field still there at Huffman Prairie, outside Dayton, or Wilbur's racetrack in France and Orville's parade grounds at Fort Myer, Virginia?

I found these places and many more. And I spent many days

at the Library of Congress, and within the archives of Dayton's Wright State University, reading thousands of letters, going through photo albums and microfilm and notebooks and ledgers—even Orville's lifelong collection of business and calling cards left by visitors. The brothers would have disapproved; they avoided attention. And they may have thought I needed to dress better—for a year I mostly wore shorts or jeans while researching the lives of two men who wore suits and stiff collars and ties, even at the workbench, even in the air. But I'm sure, had I met them, spent an hour on their front porch, they would have put me at ease with smiles and teasing laughter.

After the reading and research, after seeing where they lived and worked and flew, I found the story of the Wrights to be far more complex than I'd ever imagined. Mysteries remain. As they should.

All happiness is a kind of innocence.

MARGUERITE YOURCENAR

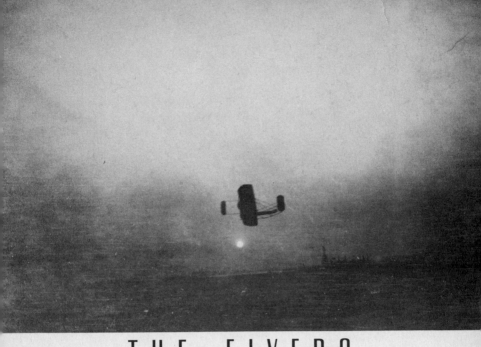

THE FLYERS

CHAPTER ONE
WOODLAND CEMETERY

"I KNOW WHERE ALL THE BODIES ARE BURIED," JIM SANDEGREN tells me, laughing, as we walk up one of the cemetery roads. He also knows the names of all the trees. This was a rural cemetery, laid out over a farmer's uncut hillsides a mile from downtown Dayton. Sandegren is the staff horticulturist. He has thirty thousand trees and a hundred thousand souls to look after.

"Here's where the Wright brothers are." He points to a granite monument with the carved family name, overlooking five graves. "People on tours especially are amazed. They expect to see something much more grand and glorious than this, and I always say that the Wrights probably felt what they did was monument enough. No two people ever lived, I mean short of Jesus, who would have had a greater impact on the numbers of people than Wilbur and Orville did."

Sandegren wears work boots and a blue-and-white striped shirt with JIM over a pocket that contains reading glasses, pen, a plastic calendar. Every day he takes a diagnostic walk through the cemetery woods, touching limbs, feathering leaves through his fingers. He says his biggest problem is keeping the trees safe from the mowers and string trimmers. The tricolor beech is a favorite—he shows me one that's a century old. Now, in midsummer, the variegated leaves have a reddish tint, soon to change to creamy pink and white, then green in the fall. And sassafras trees—one of them is an Ohio State Champion. "I have never seen the big sassafras to the extent that we have here," Sandegren says. "I love the tree. You know it was the original material for root beer? The flavoring?" He cracks off a piece of bark and a clean, lemony aroma floats out. "When we dig a grave close to a sassafras tree, invariably we'll get into the roots and they're very pungent. A lot of the guys will take them and wash them and make tea, like a spring tonic."

I ask about the gravedigger's work, how it's done these days. "We have a thirty-six-inch backhoe. Sometimes it'll be gravelly, which causes cave-ins, and you have to get down in the hole, which represents a certain amount of hazard, but nobody's going to be working by themselves."

"How deep?"

"You put thirty inches of material on top and the casket's about thirty-two inches, so roughly between five and six feet. But you've noticed these hills we've got here—sometimes you'll get eighteen inches of dirt on one end of a casket and six foot on the other."

The Wright family plot is on a slight downslope, fifty yards below a road that runs along Woodland Cemetery's top ridge. The grave markers sit together in a modest-sized rectangular space, and it would be reasonable to think of Orville standing here with a pencil and graph paper, deciding who would end up where. An engineer, drawing an airplane, sketching a gravesite—the aim is for the elegant, economical line. The family monument, shoulder-high and four feet wide, stands at the high end of the plot. The letters WRIGHT emerge from the granite front. The parents' headstones are centered in the grass below: Susan C. Wright and Milton Wright. And in a row farther on, the three children: Wilbur Wright, Katharine Wright Haskell, and Orville Wright. All the stones are small, low, and rounded—"pillow markers" they're called by cemetarians—and bear the same style of raised letters and numbers.

I'm confused about where to stand. "Where are the graves, actually?" I ask Jim. "I don't want to be standing on top of Wilbur here."

"The bodies are behind the headstones," he said. "You view the body over the headstone, so it's really a footstone."

There were two older Wright brothers, Reuchlin, buried in Kansas City, and Lorin, who's with his own family here at Woodland. And two other siblings, twins, who died in infancy. They had long lain under a single marker in another Dayton cemetery, and when the Wright descendants learned that grave was being neglected, Jim Sandegren volunteered to go dig up the remains and bring them to Woodland. He did so alone, without ceremony or publicity. He said what he found wouldn't fill a coffee can, just some discolored earth. He reburied the twins at the base of the family monument, and propped up their tombstone:

OTIS & IDA
Children of
Milton & Susan C.
WRIGHT

DIED
March 1870
ages
13 & 18 days

People often leave money on the Wrights' headstones. On this day, on Wilbur's, I count five dimes, twenty-three pennies, and a precisely placed acorn. Jim says he picks up the coins, saving them in his desk to buy flowers for the Wrights.

The grave of Paul Laurence Dunbar is in this same cemetery section, under a shimmering golden willow. Both of Dunbar's parents had been slaves in Kentucky. He was raised by his mother, Mrs. Matilda Dunbar, on Dayton's West Side, and he went to high school with Orville. The Wrights published Dunbar's earliest poetry in the weekly neighborhood newspaper they'd started in 1889, as part of their home-based printing business. Paul Dunbar became famous for his use of African-American dialect—he read for Queen Victoria in London—but felt he had more to offer in classic poetry and fiction. He died of tuberculosis, unhappy, a drinker, at thirty-three.

The Dunbar monument is a rough granite boulder, with a Tiffany-made bronze plaque now softened by verdigris, which carries a stanza of his poetry:

> Lay me down beneaf de willers in de grass,
> Whah de branch'll go a-singing as it pass;
> An' w'en I's a-layin' low
> I kin hyeah it as it go
> Singin' "Sleep, my honey, tek' yo' res' at las'."

The most visited grave at Woodland Cemetery belongs not to the Wright Brothers, or Paul Dunbar, or the beloved hometown humor columnist Erma Bombeck, but to a young boy named Johnny Morehouse. When people stop at the cemetery's main gate they most often ask—especially if they have children in the car—"Where's the Boy and his Dog?"

The answer *could* be "Take the first right and then the first left and when you start laughing you're there." Those directions will lead you to the statue of a dog, which happens on this day to be wearing surfer sunglasses. Then you notice: an American flag, an angel, a blue pinwheel, a baseball, a yellow toy dump truck, a teddy bear with a green hat, golden and purple and red plastic flowers, an assortment of big-eyed Beanie Babies—all but covering up a sleeping stone boy wearing a blue-and-white plaid tam o'shanter.

Jim says, "Kids will come and leave a toy or a bag of pebbles, special things. Sometimes they'll trade, and take something home to play with for a while."

The dog is poised in vigil, his left foreleg arched over the body of the child. The name JOHNNY MOREHOUSE is on the pedestal. Jim tells me the story: "Johnny Morehouse was a five-year-old boy in 1860 and he ran the neighborhoods freely. I've never heard anybody say what his dog's name was. Johnny was playing around the canal and got too close and got into the water and into trouble and his dog jumped in and pulled him out, but not in time to save his life. But the dog laid the boy on the ground and was so protective that he crouched over the body just like you see it in the statue and wouldn't even let the authorities touch it."

I ask, "Johnny Morehouse is really buried here?"

"Oh yes. And it was even said that later the dog would come to the cemetery and lay down beside the grave."

The City Vault is next on Jim's tour. He'll take schoolkids inside and recite poems about bats, watching the youngsters' eyes widen and gleam. He unlocks the building for me with a clank and *wheeeek* of the steel door.

"This vault is made of Dayton Formation limestone," he says. "It was built by James Wuichet in 1847 for twenty dollars, and he took that in the form of a twelve-grave lot."

The style is vaguely Egyptian, with two columns in front presuming to hold up the roof. The limestone is streaked with rain and age, returning to the earth.

We step inside. The air is dark-dusty and heavy.

"They used to keep bodies in here, you can see the brackets and beams and cleats along the side? Maybe twenty-four caskets at a time."

In the nineteenth century the winters were colder, Jim maintains, and sometimes you had to wait for a thaw so you could dig the grave. Then he pauses: "The not-so-nice explanation involves the body snatchers." People called the grave robbers "resurrectionists." They sold bodies to medical schools for study—by one physician's estimate, five thousand bodies in Ohio between 1811 and 1881. They opened the coffin, then dragged the corpse out, leaving the clothes behind, and replaced the earth and sod.

Jim says, "So what they decided was to put the deceased in this vault for two or three weeks and give the body time to deteriorate to the point where it wouldn't be of any value and then take it out and bury it."

✜   ✜

A Gypsy gravesite stands atop one of the small hills in the cemetery. There are many caskets in an underground vault, below a monument to King Levi and Queen Matilda Stanley. Levi's father, Owen Stanley, had been a Gypsy leader in England before settling in Dayton. When Queen Matilda was buried at Woodland in 1878, one newspaper counted a thousand carriages in the procession from downtown; she'd been Gypsy Queen of the United States and it was a gathering of the tribe.

"The Stanley tribe had camps and farms north of town," says Jim. "In fact, there's two streets out there, one is Gypsy Street and one is Nomad Street, and they stayed there in cold weather. In the summertime they traveled, went around door to door sharpening kitchen knives; they were tinsmiths and coopers and horse traders. The women dressed very well. They had jewelry and lots of it, and when they went out they put it all on."

Some of the older people of Dayton might steer you toward Elizabeth Richter's monument. Professionally she was known as "Lib Hedges." She owned the Bon Ton Hotel, one of twenty *maisons de joie* in Dayton in the 1890s—the names of the madams would be painted on red glass over the front doors: Cleo LaBelle, Ferne DeMarr, Flo Dowdie . . . It is said that Lib Hedges—generous with charities and flood relief—was worth half a million dollars when she died. She invested in real estate and took pride in finding houses for her girls when they left to be married. She also provided burial benefits when there was no known family, and now alongside Ms. Hedges's monument at Woodland are two small headstones bearing only the names Lora and Maud.

Jim and I walk on, past the graves of nineteen Revolutionary War veterans, past the curving ranks of Civil War headstones, past the old potter's field, called the Dayton City Lot. On every hillside can be found victims of the Great Flood of 1913, and the influenza epidemic in 1918. And you'll recognize the prominent Dayton names: Charles Kettering invented the automobile self-starter, for Cadillac. John Patterson perfected the selling of cash registers and led NCR into a data-processing future. Former Ohio governor James Cox founded a chain of newspapers and radio and TV stations. George Huffman made sewing machines, then Huffy bicycles. In the community of spirit that is Woodland Cemetery, the Wright brothers are among their peers. Dayton, Ohio, in 1900, led the nation in per capita patent grants.

As I walk the narrow cemetery roadways in the afternoon's slanting light, I am reminded of the tragedy of Wilbur's death. His hearse, drawn by white horses, passed along this way, after an open-casket viewing in a downtown church. The *Dayton Daily News* reported, "Thousands Follow Sad Cortege." His brother Orville said that day, "Wilbur had plans that no one will be able to carry into execution."

Of the three youngest Wrights, Wilbur was the first to die, at forty-five. And his life had been just about to change—the difficult, often dangerous years of developing and testing and selling airplanes would be coming to an end.

In the spring of 1911, the year before his death, Wilbur traveled to England, France, then Germany, fulfilling the Wrights' contracts to train pilots, and watching after several patent-infringement lawsuits. He was angered by "scoundrels and thieves" who would attempt to steal the brothers' ideas, and he wrote Orville in June to say that if it weren't for the patent fights and their obligation to investors, he'd be ready to quit. "If I could get free from business with the money we already have in hand I would rather do it than continue in business at a considerable profit."

Wilbur was tired of traveling, and he missed his family. In 1911 he wrote from Berlin to his sister Katharine: "The papers report temperatures ranging from 105 to 110 degrees in America. I hope you have got poor old daddy's fan going for him all night. . . . Don't let him shut off the fan during the nights to save money. . . ."

I found a sparse but moving narrative of Wilbur's final months in Bishop Wright's *Diaries: 1857–1917,* a volume that runs to 850 pages. The bishop kept notes in a long succession of small, leatherbound journals. He'd remark on his travels and his preaching, his sons' aviation endeavors, Katharine's teaching career, and who came to dinner and what they talked about. These are among the entries that lead up to and culminate with his son's death:

Monday, January 1, 1912: "It is a bright cool-like day. This is the eighty-fourth First Day of the Year I have seen. They have been years of toil, but little physical pain. Not a year has been devoid of much happiness."

Thursday, January 11: "Wilbur went in the afternoon to New York City."

Saturday, January 13: "I was cleaning up my closet. Katharine went to Columbus, to visit the College Club. She reached home at midnight. I sat up till she came home. The mercury ran down to about zero."

Thursday, April 18: ". . . the number lost on the *Titanic* seems larger than before. Wilbur started to New York to make a contract with the Aero Club."

Thursday, May 2: "Wilbur began to have typhoid fever; first diagnosed, by Dr. D. B. Conklin, as probably malarial fever, and later as a typhoidal fever."

Tuesday, May 7: "Wilbur is better. But still has considerable fever."

Friday, May 10: "I took Lorin . . . we staid to see the Ringling parade. . . . Many wagons and nice horses, several open carriages with bears, wild cats, hyenas, leopards, tigers, lions and lionesses. A dozen camels, twenty odd elephants, a steam whistle. Wilbur still has high fever."

Sunday, May 12: "Wilbur continues the same. His fever rises in the afternoon. . . . The doctor called twice."

Wednesday, May 15: Wilbur has not as high fever as some days. Roosevelt spoke in Dayton, to-night, and Orville went to hear him, but was crowded out, and heard a suffraget."

Thursday, May 16: "Wilbur's fever is unchanged. Orville left for Washington City, at 9:00, to deliver a machine to the government."

Saturday, May 18: "Wilbur is not better. He has an attack mentally, for the worse. It was a bad spell. He is put under opiates. He is unconscious mostly."

Tuesday, May 21: "The doctors came at 7:30, thought Wilbur had held his own."

Friday, May 24: "Wilbur seems, in nearly every respect, better. The doctors have a long examination before noon."

Monday, May 27: "His fever was higher and he has difficulty with the bladder. . . . I slept with my clothes on. We thought him near death."

Wednesday, May 29: "Wilbur seemed no worse, though he had a chill. The fever was down, but rose high. He remained the same til 3:15 in the morning, when, eating his allowance, he expired, without a struggle."

Thursday, May 30: "This morning at 3:15, Wilbur passed away, aged 45 years, 1 month, and 14 days."

Monday, June 3: "Wilbur is dead and buried! We are all stricken. It does not seem possible that he is gone. Probably Orville and Katharine felt his loss most. They say little."

It had been Wilbur's idea to try to build an airplane. In May of 1899 he wrote to the Smithsonian Institution in Washington for information:

I have been interested in the problem of mechanical and human flight ever since as a boy I constructed a number of bats of various sizes after the style of [Sir George] Cayley and [Alphonse] Pénaud's machines. My observations since have only convinced me more firmly that human flight is possible and practicable. . . . I am about to begin a systematic study of the subject in preparation for practical work to which I expect to devote what time I can spare from my regular business. I wish to obtain such papers as the Smithsonian Institution has published on this subject. . . . I am an enthusiast, but not a crank in the sense that I have some pet theories as to the proper construction of a flying machine. I wish to avail myself of all that is already known and then if possible add my mite to help on the future worker who will attain final success.

Wilbur's second letter to the Secretary of the Smithsonian is dated June 14, and he thanks him for sending a list of selected books on aerial navigation and pamphlets numbered 903, 938, 1134, and 1135 from the Smithsonian *Reports.* "I enclose one dollar currency for which you may send me *Experiments in Aerodynamics* [by] Langley."

Mr. Langley, the author, was indeed Samuel P. Langley, the Secretary of the Smithsonian; the correspondence with Wilbur Wright had been handled by his assistant. And Langley's experiments represented America's official aviation research project. With the Smithsonian's money, he'd built a series of small model aircraft, finally achieving success in 1896 with Aerodrome Number 5—a frail craft with a fourteen-foot wingspan and steam-driven twin propellers that circled out over the Potomac River in a ninety-second flight. Langley was determined to build a version that was big enough to carry a pilot, and the U.S. Army gave him $50,000 to make the try. (Langley's Great Aerodrome, with Charles Manly aboard, made its second and final disastrous plunge into the river on December 8, 1903, less than two weeks before the Wrights' first flight at Kitty Hawk.)

At Woodland Cemetery, standing under the oaks and hickory, sumac and wild black cherry, Jim Sandegren, keeper of stories as well as trees, tells me what he's come to realize about the Wrights. "They considered themselves a nuclear family, 'the five of us against the world.' They felt the world was full of cheaters and liars and they had to stick together; they were the only ones they could depend on."

Bishop Milton Wright's life was perhaps the most fulfilled. His sons earned hometown respect and worldwide acclaim. His daughter graduated from Oberlin at a time when barely two percent of young women went to college. He won most of his fights—on matters of dogma and principle—with the United Brethren Church. The bishop stayed healthy and preached and read books and went for walks until his eighty-seventh year.

And once he flew in an airplane. In the spring of 1910 he went up with Orville over Huffman Prairie, outside Dayton. A fine photograph exists from that moment, showing the sketchy lines of a biplane aloft on a cloudy day, moving toward the camera. You can make out two people on the lower wing, and you can cheer for Milton Wright because he said, "Higher, Orville, higher!" Also this day, for the first and only time, Orville and Wilbur went for a flight together. It was something they had long ago promised their father they would never do surely so that no single accident could kill both. Of all the bishop's diary entries, this may well be the most understated:

Wednesday, May 25: "It is a nice day. Invitations come from Coin, Iowa, to attend June 2, the graduating exercises of High School (Mabel Harris), and from Basehor, Kan., Grammar School (Bertha Wright). Wrote letter to each. Mrs. LaShapelle called. We all went to Sim[m]s Station. Orville rose 1600 and 2600 feet in flights. Orville & Wilbur took a first flight together. Orville took me up 350 feet and 6.55 minutes.

✛   ✛

After the bishop died in 1917—five years after Wilbur's passing—Orville and Katharine remained in their new home,
Hawthorn Hill. They entertained as a couple, they traveled
together—it was as if they had pledged not to separate. But
eventually Katharine fell in love with one of her Oberlin class-
mates, kept it secret for as long as she could bear, and then, at
fifty-two, married Henry J. Haskell, an editor of the *Kansas City
Star*. She'd been fearful of telling Orville, and her concern was
justified. Orville refused to attend the wedding. Two years later,
when Katharine lay dying of pneumonia, Orville had to be
urged to go to her bedside. He arrived on a Saturday, she died
Sunday evening. He brought his sister back to Dayton for the
funeral, and burial in the family plot. Three military airplanes
circled low over Woodland Cemetery and dropped roses on
Katharine Wright Haskell's grave.

Orville lived by himself at Hawthorn Hill for two more
decades, through and past World War II, long enough to see the
new dimensions of flight. Chuck Yeager broke the sound barrier in the X-1 rocket plane over the Mojave Desert. "Yeager,"
the air force had told him, "this is the airplane to fly. It will be
the most historic ride since the Wright Brothers." Orville was
briefed on the secret flight, and he must have smiled in wonder:
the X-1 flew at Mach 1.07—700 miles an hour. Chuck Yeager
had trained at Wright Field in Dayton, and, like the Wrights,
lacked a college engineering degree, but he didn't worry much
about the experts who said that airplanes would break apart
when they neared the speed of sound. A technical note from
Yeager's flight could apply to the arc of the Wrights' career as

well: The pilot who breaks the sound barrier doesn't hear the sonic boom—it's left behind as he flies on.

Orville Wright died of heart failure at age seventy-seven, and his burial completed the family gravesite. On that day, February 2, 1948, the city schools were closed at noon. Four U.S. Air Force jets flew down the valley from nearby Wright-Patterson field to soar past in the "missing man" formation, in tribute to America's first pilot.

From this ridge along the north side of Woodland Cemetery— the highest point in Dayton—you can see the tall buildings arrayed along the lines of the rivers and creeks. I watch the breeze sweeping through the trees, tossing up the pale under- sides of the oak leaves, thinking of how this story ends, with the quiet simplicity of these five nearby graves, and how it begins— with the wind.

CHAPTER TWO

TO KITTY HAWK

CROSSING THE VIRGINIA–NORTH CAROLINA STATE LINE, I drove south on U.S. 17, alongside the Dismal Swamp Canal. Wilbur came by train, the Norfolk & Southern. I had an overnight bag on the backseat, Wilbur had a trunk full of tools and wire and cotton fabric in the baggage car. We both arrived in Elizabeth City in early evening. We both walked to the town dock. We were both looking for Kitty Hawk.

The view from the waterfront is to the southeast, down the wide reach of the Pasquotank River as it flows out into Albemarle Sound. On the map you can draw a straight line from here to the Outer Banks, but all you can see is water—Kitty Hawk is thirty-two miles away, down the river, across the sound, into the mists of the Atlantic Ocean.

On September 5, 1900, Katharine had written to her father, who was traveling: "We are in an uproar getting Will off. The trip will do him good. I don't think he will be reckless. If they can arrange it, Orv will go down as soon as Will has the machine ready."

Bishop Milton Wright had been informed about this, two days earlier, in a letter from Wilbur: "I am intending to start in a few days for a trip to the coast of North Carolina in the vicinity of Roanoke Island, for the purpose of making some experiments with a flying machine. . . . At any rate, I shall have an outing of several weeks and see a part of the world I have never before visited."

Wilbur's desire to travel would have made sense to his father. Milton Wright, as a church missionary in his late twenties, had seen Philadelphia and New York, had sailed to Panama and then up the West Coast to San Francisco and Portland, Oregon. The brothers had only been on one long trip, visiting the Chicago World's Fair in 1893.

The first train ride to North Carolina began on a Thursday evening. Wilbur left Dayton on the Big Four Route—running between Cincinnati, Cleveland, Chicago, and St. Louis. The Chesapeake & Ohio Railway carried him from Cincinnati to the far southeast of Virginia. Through the night, the train sped along the Kentucky side of the Ohio River, with brief stops in Maysville, South Portsmouth, Russell, Ashland, and Catlettsburg. Crossing into West Virginia, the route left the Ohio behind and found the Kanawha River, near Charleston, then turned south into the New River Gorge.

The C&O had blasted and carved space for the tracks alongside the New River in the 1870s, making it worthwhile to mine coal in the gorge. A train passenger in the dark of early morning would not have seen the cliffs rising a thousand feet above the water, or noticed much about the coal towns—Nuttall, Sewell, Fire Creek—that were signaled with a pull of the steam whistle. Thurmond was at the center of the railroad coal traffic, one busy street alongside the tracks, and Wilbur's train did stop there, at 4:22 A.M. An hour farther on, at Hinton, the route turned east, passing through the Big Bend Tunnel, where John Henry's steel-driving legend began.

The train met sunrise not far from the resort town of White Sulphur Springs. Then the Virginia border and on to Charlottesville at lunchtime, leaving the mountains behind. Richmond was the next city, then Williamsburg, Newport News, Hampton, and finally Old Point Comfort. Wilbur stepped off his train at about 6:00 P.M. and could see and smell the ocean.

He collected his luggage, his airplane parts, and, as he wrote, "went over to Norfolk via the steamer *Pennsylvania*. Put up at the Monticello Hotel. Spent Saturday morning trying to find spruce for spars of machine, but was unsuccessful. Finally I bought some white pine and had it sawed up at J. E. Etheridge Co. mill. Cumpston Goffigon, the foreman, very accommodating. The weather was near 100 Fahr. And I nearly collapsed. At 4:30 left for Eliz. City and put up at the Arlington where I spent several days waiting for a boat to Kitty Hawk. No one seemed to know anything about the place or how to get there."

Wilbur had been told he could catch the weekly freight boat that ran to Manteo on Roanoke Island, near Kitty Hawk, but it sailed the day before he arrived. He wouldn't have worked on Sunday; the brothers never did. On Monday he bought supplies and sorted out his gear. On Tuesday morning he encountered Israel Perry, owner of the fishing schooner *Curlicue*, and, for three dollars, "engaged passage" to Kitty Hawk.

✛   ✛

On a map of the United States, the Outer Banks are just the sketch of a pencil, a line of thin islands curving down from Virginia to midcoast North Carolina. At some points they lie so far off the mainland as to suggest a seagoing existence for the people who live there. In former times a small farm would shelter back in the sand dunes and oak woods, on a mile-wide stretch of land between the ocean and the vast and shallow bodies of water known as sounds—Currituck, Albemarle, Roanoke, and Pamlico. The North Carolina rivers brought rainfall down from the mountains, into the sounds and then the sea. The water cut openings between islands—they're called inlets, though "outlet" is the truer description. A cargo schooner down from Boston or Baltimore, bound for mainland ports, would require a local man who knew the way the inlets would sand up and shift. Piloting became a paying job, and the early settlements grew up around the inlets.

The people—mostly English in heritage—came from other parts of North Carolina and other states, and from the ships of the world passing by or wrecking. They lived in weather and isolation, and were stronger for it. Even the names in the cemeteries suggest purpose: Guard, Foreman, Gallop, Outlaw, Fearing, Silverthorne, Jewell and Brite, Hayman, Tiller, Twiford, Basnight.

The schooner *Henrietta Pierce* went aground off the Outer Banks and was lost in 1853. The steamer *Metropolis* went down in 1878. The *Ada F. Whitney,* 1885. The *Josie Troop,* a Canadian bark, 1889. The *Eagle,* 1870. On the same quarter-mile of coast: the *Hattie Lollis,* the *Patriot,* the *Adamantine,* the *Laura Nelson,* the *Harvest,* and the *Voucher.*

The storms rise offshore of the islands, where the warm Gulf Stream waters meet colder flows from the north. Unseen shoals reach far out into the Atlantic. Ship captains wanting to keep the coast in sight found no leeway in gale-force seas. Hundreds of ships have foundered on the shoals, broken apart, lost cargo and crew.

New professions were born on the Outer Banks. Lighthouse builders, lighthouse keepers. And the U.S. Life-Saving Service built stations at the beach. The surfmen walked patrols through the night. They carried signal pistols—a red flare from the beach gave hope to the captain of an endangered vessel. The lifesaving crews brought their equipment on a cart, pushing it through the deep sands. A heavy brass cannon fired a shot line into a ship's rigging for a "breeches buoy" rescue—a pair of canvas trousers attached to a flotation device. Or the surfboat was launched, with six men rowing and one steering as they fought through and over the crashing waves. "Women, children, and helpless persons" were taken ashore first.

The stationkeeper, who ran the rescue operations and captained the surfboat, and who was paid the most—$900 was the salary for the year 1903—also had to sit down with his pen and fill out the official Wreck Report. "Name of Vessel . . . Date of Disaster . . . Hailing-port and nationality . . . Nature of cargo . . . State of wind and weather . . . Number of trips with surf-boat . . . Number of persons brought ashore with breeches-buoy . . ." Sixty-seven questions in all, with the critical ones on the last page: "Number of lives saved . . . Number of lives lost . . . Estimated value of cargo saved . . . Number of persons sheltered at station, how long, and total number of meals furnished . . . Number and names of persons resuscitated from apparent death by drowning or exposure to cold . . . Number of persons found after death and cared for."

✣   ✣

In 1900, the first year the Wrights went to North Carolina, they needed to see if their new full-size glider would fly. Wilbur had built a five-foot biplane kite the year before, developing his theory of wing warping as a way to turn in the air, while still maintaining balance. His model was a bird in flight, especially the changing angle of its wingtips: One tilted up in the air current and the other one down, "turning itself into an animated windmill." As Wilbur wrote many years later, "Here was the silent birth of all that underlies human flight." To test the first glider, the Wrights needed a constant strong wind, a treeless landscape, the elevations of small hills, and sand for safe landings.

September was the time available; the bicycle shop would be busy until then. Wilbur wrote to Octave Chanute, the Chicago engineer and aeronautical enthusiast. Chanute's experimental gliders had flown from the Indiana Dunes, on Lake Michigan's shore, but he'd had troublesome experiences with newspaper reporters coming out from the city. San Diego and Pine Island, Florida, Chanute knew, had "steady sea breezes," but both lacked sand hills. Wilbur asked the U.S. Weather Bureau for advice, and was sent the average hourly wind tables from stations all across the country. Kitty Hawk ranked sixth in wind intensity.

By late summer Wilbur had this letter from William J. Tate, of Kitty Hawk, who had been the postmaster and whose wife, Addie, currently held the job:

> Mr. J. J. Dosher of the Weather Bureau here has asked me to answer your letter to him, relative to the fitness of Kitty Hawk as a place to practice or experiment with a flying machine, etc. In answering I would say that you

would find here nearly any type of ground you could wish; you could, for instance, get a stretch of sandy land one mile by five with a bare hill in center 80 feet high, not a tree or a bush anywhere to break the evenness of the wind current. Our winds are always steady, generally from 10 to 20 miles velocity per hour. . . . We have telegraph communication and daily mails. Climate healthy, you could find good place to pitch tents & get board in private family providing there were not too many in your party. . . . Don't wait until November. The autumn generally gets a little rough by November. . . . I assure you you will find a hospitable people when you come among us.

At sunset, early in still-warm November 2002, 102 years later, I walked the quiet streets of Elizabeth City, watching the gold and red cloud layers coming in from the west, and the reflected gleam on the calm surface of the Pasquotank. Elizabeth City has an old downtown, with buildings of softened brick that carry the original business names in fading paint: Hessons's Department Store, Rose City Milling Company. Once—before bridges—this was the port city for the Outer Banks; people would arrive by boat and stay over Saturday night. They'd shop for a month's groceries, have supper in a restaurant, go to the movies.

Wilbur's Arlington Hotel is gone, replaced by a three-story condominium, the La Casita. I put up at the Comfort Inn, out at the bypass. I had plans for my own boat trip, leaving at first light.

At the Pelican Marina the next morning, Enno Reckendorf gives me a hand as I step over the side of his twenty-five-foot power boat, *Miss Martha*. Captain Reckendorf is a retired school administrator, sturdy, with a trim white beard. He wears a fleece-lined red plaid jacket and has amber shades over his bifocals. He says, "We're going up sun, I call it. On the way back it'll be down sun."

Enno has a green steel thermos of coffee and a small cooler with his lunch. I've brought water and a cheese sandwich. We'll be out for most of the day's light. I've asked to go to Kitty Hawk Bay. "Can't quite get that far and back to the dock before dark," he says, "but we'll be in sight of it."

Miss Martha's diesel engine finds a comfortable rumble, as we head off into the Pasquotank. The wake behind us is a brown and white churn. Enno holds the throttle at seven and a half knots, checks our progress on his portable GPS unit, drinks coffee. We are in the deep channel in the center of the river, heading east-southeast. Graceful, white-painted homes are on both sides, amid cedars and pines.

Unlike mine, Wilbur Wright's journey down the Pasquotank in September 1900 began with some strenuous rowing: "As [the *Curlicue*] was anchored about three miles down the river we started in his skiff, which was loaded almost to the gunwale with three men, my heavy trunk and lumber. The boat leaked very badly and frequently dipped water, but by constant bailing we managed to reach the schooner in safety. The weather was very fine with a light west wind blowing."

A local sailor, George Jackson, talking with me about Wilbur's account, said, "It is odd that the boat would be three miles down the Pasquotank. First, that's a hell of a row, particularly with supplies. And Elizabeth City exists because of its deep-water location at the narrows of the river. A boat doesn't need to be that far out. I don't think Israel Perry would have left his boat there unless he was trying to sneak into town."

Somewhere in a past decade, the *Curlicue* was lost, becoming woodsmoke or a backyard shed, or left moldering at the bottom of the sound. No pictures exist of her. George Jackson owns an old-style wooden skipjack, and he feels sure that Perry's boat had a centerboard—a keel panel that you can raise in shallow water—even though Wilbur described it as being "flat-bottomed." Jackson has respect for the watermen of the sound: "It gets dreadful in weather. The waves get steep, and the spits and shoals go out for miles. I've been sunk twice out there."

Aboard *Miss Martha,* propelled by her sixty-horsepower diesel, Enno Reckendorf and I reach the three-mile mark after twenty-five minutes. To make it this far in a leaking loaded rowboat seems improbable. Elizabeth City is a shimmer behind us. The river widens. The chart shows a ten-foot depth and indicates we're in a seaplane-operating area. It's an outdated designation. The coast guard has an air station on the south bank, and instead of seaplanes we see rising flights of four-engine C-130 Hercules transports. They take off downriver, then circle for touch-and-go landings. I sit back on the pilothouse cushions, watching the ducks float on the water and the trees on the bank slide slowly past, recalling Wilbur's reaction when he climbed on board the *Curlicue*: "When I mounted the deck of the larger boat I discovered at a glance that it was in worse condition if possible than the skiff. The sails were rotten, the ropes badly worn and the rudderpost half rotted off, and the cabin so dirty and vermin-infested that I kept out of it from first to last. The wind became very light, making progress slow."

Farther along the river a blimp appears, tilting into the sky at a sharp upward angle. It's light gray, elegant in its movements.

Enno says, "That's a blimp outfit. It's commercial now, used to be the Naval Air Station." The impossibly large, silver-colored curved hangar comes into sight. "You can see that from miles away, down in Albemarle Sound."

The company, called TCOM, makes and maintains helium-filled lighter-than-air craft 195 feet long. If Fuji wants a majestic white-and-green blimp to fly around the country advertising color film, the work's done inside this huge building. During World War II, navy blimps patrolled the Outer Banks coastline, protecting shipping lanes from German submarine attacks.

As we leave the Pasquotank River, moving on into Albemarle Sound, the view from the bow of *Miss Martha* is of an ocean horizon. If there is land to be seen, today it is lost in haze. At this point in his trip, Wilbur Wright would have been looking directly at the Outer Banks, at the low rise of land above Kitty Hawk Bay. On a stormy day he may have doubted that land lay ahead.

From his writing: "Though we had started immediately after dinner it was almost dark when we passed out of the mouth of the Pasquotank and headed down the sound. The water was much rougher than the light wind would have led us to expect, and Israel spoke of it several times and seemed a little uneasy. . . . The waves which were now running quite high struck the boat from below with a heavy shock and threw it back about as fast as it went forward. The leeway was greater than the headway."

Enno pulls our boat alongside the derelict Wade Point Light. Wilbur would have passed this light station and seen it manned and lit. Wade Point was a "screwpile" light, standing alone out in the sound. Tall poles with steel blades at the bottom were twisted into the firm ground of a shoal, and a lighthouse was constructed on a platform above the water. It looked like a summer cottage, with white picket railing all around. The light stood atop the peaked roof. The keeper lived "aboard" with his family. For ninety-nine years fishermen and boat captains who sailed these uncertain waters knew Wade Point to be a white light, steady and visible on a clear night from eleven nautical miles away.

We swing clear of the lighthouse remains—the pilings and the collapsing steel frame, now a streaked and stained perch for cormorants and pelicans—with radar reflectors nailed up to warn approaching boat traffic. I leave with a vision of Wade Point's past—decades of long, anxious nights spent on duty here, with nor'easters ripping past the shuttered windows, the keeper in the top gallery ringing the fog bell, his wife below in quarters, reading to the children by lamplight.

There was also once a lighthouse nearby on land, at the entrance to North River, which is coming up on our left. It's a big river, coming into Albemarle Sound, but Enno says, "If we wanted to go up there we'd have a tiny passage to aim for." He points to the chart. We are motoring with *Miss Martha* over water that is shown in white, with depths of ten to thirteen feet. Turn toward the wide and inviting North River mouth and soon you're in the blue area of the chart, in water that is one to four feet deep. Boaters must follow a straight line right up the center.

At this spot in the sound in 1900, Wilbur was helping bail water from Israel Perry's schooner: "At 11 o'clock the wind had increased to a gale and the boat was gradually being driven nearer and nearer the north shore, but as an attempt to turn round would probably have resulted in an upset there seemed nothing else to do but attempt to round the North River light and take refuge behind the point. In a severe gust the foresail was blown loose from the boom and fluttered to leeward with a terrible roar."

Somehow the *Curlicue* made it into North River. Wilbur slept on deck. The next day the storm let up, but the boat was a mess, and it was past dark before they reached the calm of Kitty Hawk Bay. This was almost home for Captain Perry, who fished from Collington Island, on the bay's southern edge. The waters near the shore are marshy, with hidden channels even today marked by the locals. "Honor the marks," a fisherman would say. "Don't go past the pole with the deer antlers. Turn when you see a cougar tail and two red reflectors nailed up."

Enno Reckendorf's GPS unit tells us we've traveled twenty-five nautical miles out from the Pelican Marina. We've reached a red triangle atop a piling—"2P" on the chart. To the southeast the sand dunes of Jockey's Ridge State Park are shining white in the sun. With binoculars, I have a clear view of the Wright Monument—the granite pylon atop Big Kill Devil Hill. Kitty Hawk is ahead to the east, a low shadow of land against the blue of the Atlantic sky.

We're at our turnaround point, and it's time for lunch. Enno cuts the engine and the boat drifts free. The wind is down and the air is moist, cold, and clear. We talk about the storms that come up quickly on the sound. This water is more dangerous than the open ocean, Enno says. "You're fishing offshore and the wind moves the water in long swells. Here, it's shallow and the waves come quicker and steeper—it's like riding a hobby horse." In 1999, he says, Hurricane Floyd sent a tidal surge flooding up the Pasquotank River. People in the area will tell you, "The blue crabs were eatin' the collard greens that day."

For dessert I offer Enno spoonfuls of strawberry preserves on bread. He knows the story about Wilbur Wright, that all he ate during his two-day trip down from Elizabeth City was a small jar of homemade jam that Katharine had put in his luggage. Ours is a small tribute to an adventure on this water over a century ago.

Red painted letters on a wooden sign by the driveway: STICK. David Stick told me on the phone that his house was down by the water, at the end of Elijah Baum Road. Baum was the youngster who welcomed Wilbur Wright to the Outer Banks.

A second night had been spent aboard the *Curlicue,* with Wilbur again trying to sleep on deck. He went ashore in the morning, September 17. Elijah, people like to say, was there crabbing in the water. He talked with Wilbur, then walked him up the sandy path to the post office, where Bill and Addie Tate lived.

In 1900 Kitty Hawk was a bayside collection of houses, a store, a church. It was the center for trade and travel to the mainland. After the first road was paved in 1929, Kitty Hawk started to turn away from the water, with trucks delivering goods instead of boats. And David Stick now owns a house that Elijah Baum built for his son in 1945. It's gray with blue shutters; a wide back lawn faces the sound.

"This is about the way it looked to Wilbur when he first stepped ashore," David Stick says. "Some of these live oak trees are the exact same ones—I have pictures from the old days."

"Isn't there a new monument here, to mark the spot where Wilbur arrived?"

"It's next door at my neighbor's—the Bald View Bed and Breakfast. I asked them to put it over there. I didn't want a whole bunch of people to come wandering through here. I felt a little guilty because I've pressed so hard to have the historic sites preserved."

David Stick is eighty-two. He has long been a writer, and he continues his work in Outer Banks history. He tells me he's been trying to get the National Park Service to cut down trees at the Wright Memorial so people can have a better sense of how things looked in the early 1900s.

His father, Frank Stick, a nationally known calendar and magazine illustrator, had donated land for the Kill Devil Hills memorial. "In the mid-1920s my father was totally fed up with painting for pay, and quit at the height of his profession. He'd been coming down here from New Jersey and liked it, so he started buying property."

David Stick remembers the memorial's groundbreaking ceremony, on December 17, 1928, the twenty-fifth anniversary of the first flight: "I was eight years old. We drove down from New Jersey and took the ferry across from Point Harbor to Kitty Hawk—that's where the bridge is now. Orville Wright was there that day, but I recall a lot more about Amelia Earhart. She was lovely. I knew she was special. We rode together in the back of a pickup truck and she held on to my arm to keep me from bouncing out."

From David Stick's back porch the view is south, and every December 17 he can watch the parade of planes flying over Big Kill Devil Hill in honor of the Wrights. And at night he sees the pure white beam of the monument's beacon, swinging out across Kitty Hawk Bay.

On October 4, 1900, Katharine Wright wrote to her father, "I have not heard from the boys since last Friday, which was before Orv had got to Kitty Hawk. Probably the mail goes out but once a week. I never did hear of such an out-of-the-way place."

In traveling to the spot they'd picked out in North Carolina, Wilbur and Orville had left streetcars and telephones and factories and gone back half a century in time. There'd long been a resort hotel and summer cottages at Nags Head, but that was a distant eight miles away from Kitty Hawk. At the Outer Banks History Center, I listened to Elijah Baum as an old man, his voice recorded by his grandson for a 1961 college history project. He spoke of his mother tucking him in bed under a mosquito canopy. Of carrying oil lamps from room to room. Of houses built from wood sticks and cement made from sand and lime that came from burning oyster shells. A man would come around selling sewing machines. People usually had a few sheep and cattle back in the woods, and they'd register their brands at the courthouse. Mr. Baum remembered "the flying boys" and said years later, he helped find boards from the old hangar to mark where their flights began.

Orville soon arrived from Dayton, bringing camping gear, coffee and tea. The glider was being assembled in the Tates' front yard, with Wilbur using Addie's sewing machine on the porch. They both stayed on for a week with Bill and Addie, who'd been providing Wilbur with boiled drinking water. He told them, "I stand in mortal dread of typhoid fever, and while I am here would like to have a gallon of water boiled each morning and put in the pitcher in my room. That is all the extras I will require." He'd seen Orville suffer through the fever and delirium of typhoid four years earlier (and would himself eventually die of the disease).

It's possible to imagine a conversation at the Tates' house at dusk, the brothers sitting on the front steps with Bill and Addie, the two young girls playing nearby. Wilbur and Orville are dressed in business suits and ties, the Tates in homemade clothes, sunburned. They talk aeronautical theory, describing how they've set up the glider. Bill Tate might be talking about his father, who froze to death after being capsized in Albemarle Sound, or explaining how the local people felt about flying. As Tate said later, "At the time the Wrights arrived in our community we were set in our ways. We believed in a good God, a bad Devil, and a hot hell, and more than anything else we believed that the same good God did not believe man should ever fly."

The brothers set up their cots and gasoline stove in a white tent on a slight slope of a nearby sandy hill. It was time to test the glider. On October 14, Orville wrote Katharine: "We have been having a fine time, altogether we have had the machine out three different days. . . . Monday night and all day Tuesday we had a terrific wind blowing 36 miles an hour. Wednesday morning the Kitty Hawkers were out early peering around the edge of the woods and out of their upstairs windows to see whether our camp was still in existence. We were all right, however, and though wind continued up to 30 miles, got the machine out to give it another trial."

The glider was flown first as a kite, guided by four cords. In strong winds they put chains on it, to add weight. Wilbur made some tentative flights as a pilot, lying flat on the bottom wing. He was trying to learn—he could teach his brother later. Then they started launching from the top of a high dune at Kill Devil Hills, three miles to the south. Wilbur had a sixty-foot glide from there, and, on October 19, skimmed down the hill for a final flight of perhaps four hundred feet.

Their vacation time was ending. The glider was abandoned to the sand, and later Addie Tate used the white sateen fabric to make dresses for her two young daughters. Wilbur and Orville packed their trunks for the return to Dayton.

Orville had been writing to Katharine about the sand and the wind and the beauty of the sunsets, about the impossibility of buying fish in a fishing village, about running after chicken hawks and squirrels and having a wild goose dinner at the Tates'. His letters home from this time were vibrant and happy:

> We need no introduction in Kitty Hawk. Every place we go we are called Mr. Wright. Our fame has spread far and wide up and down the beach.
>
> It is now after eight and "time to be abed." A cold nor'easter is blowing tonight. . . . We each of us have two blankets, but almost freeze every night. The wind blows in on my head, and I pull the blankets up over my head, when my feet freeze, and I reverse the process. I keep this up all night and in the morning am hardly able

to tell "where I'm at" in the bedclothes. . . . In spite of all these little drawbacks, I have been getting in from nine to ten hours of sleep every night—except the storm nights. There is no news here, except that Mr. Calhoun the storekeeper has just sold out and will leave Kitty Hawk tomorrow. He is the most interesting character I have found here. He is an old man, broken down in health, who came here to seek recovery. "It was the greatest mistake of my life," he always tells you, "and I will die here before I am able to get away." He was not greatly beloved by the Kitty Hawkers, but was pretty well liked by us foreigners. I'm out of paper. Will start Tuesday for home.

"Ullam" is in bed asleep while I'm writing.

Before I left Kitty Hawk Village, I walked along the roads that curve through the woods. A multitude of houses have been built, and in some spots I could hear the speeding traffic from out on the main highway, but you can still see remnants of the dunes and find a clear view down to the bay.

Old photographs help: the one the Wrights made of seven resolute men and their dog at the nearby lifesaving station, or an image of a village farm couple, white-haired, she in a long dress, he in suspenders, on the porch of their unpainted house.

In the fall of 1900, Wilbur Wright was thirty-three years old, Orville twenty-nine. They were single, intent, highly competent. They had ventured from the Midwest to Kitty Hawk in much the same spirit as the people who had first settled here. Something new was possible out on the edge of the Carolinas. The life you made was mostly what you decided it would be, however hard, however lonely. The brothers wanted to build and fly a plane; somewhere in their quiet thoughts it was already in the air. On the Outer Banks they found the weather and the open land they needed, and the chance to live almost solitary lives among people they respected. They returned with improved gliders in 1901 and 1902, and the powered machine in 1903. It is difficult to think the first flight could have happened anywhere else.

CHAPTER THREE

PILOTS AND PLANES

I KNEW THAT TO BEGIN TO UNDERSTAND WHAT BROUGHT THE Wrights to the Outer Banks, again and again, to carry their glider again and again up the slopes of sand—I had to get up into the air myself, if only for the briefest of moments. So I signed up for a hang-gliding lesson.

I stood on the crest of a dune at Jockey's Ridge State Park, less than a mile from the beach at Kill Devil Hills, with a hang-gliding instructor and two young men from County Sligo, Ireland. Padraic and Michael and I constituted the Kitty Hawk Kites 1:30 P.M. class, taught by Steve Bernier, who was deeply tanned and taut after a long season helping launch the flights, chasing down the dunes, and climbing back up with the glider. He was barefoot, and I winced when he lifted his foot to extract a spiky sandspur he'd picked up from a defensive little dune plant. "You have to watch out for these, but I like the heat and the feel of the sand."

Hang gliding is a sport that began as a science, and as a pre-decessor to powered flight. Aeronautical pioneers—risk-takers to be sure—believed that if they could soar off a hillside sus-pended beneath a wing, they would simply have to install an engine and propellers and they'd invent the airplane. Otto Lilienthal, in Germany, became well known for his long, gliding flights, and then for his death in 1896, when he broke his neck after a stall and a crash. Octave Chanute designed multiwing hang-gliders and used assistants to test-fly them with no loss of life. The modern, safer flexible flying wing was designed by a Virginia engineer named Francis Rogallo. His wife, Gertrude, cut the fabric and helped assemble the kites, which they tested together in the winds of the Outer Banks. The Rogallo wing made hang gliding practical, and soon popular worldwide. Kitty Hawk Kites started flight training at Jockey's Ridge in 1974, and now instructs thousands of people every year. There are few physical requirements: You have to weigh at least eighty-five pounds and no more than 225, and "You must be able to run approximately ten yards."

Our lesson began with a video, showing hang gliders five thousand feet in the air, coming off Grandfather Mountain in western North Carolina. And scenes from here at Jockey's Ridge, with some students soaring and some stalling, with a drop to the sand. We signed waivers indemnifying Kitty Hawk Kites against various mishaps, including "loss of life," were fit-ted with chest harnesses, picked out helmets, and headed for the hill. Steve lifted our white delta-wing glider on his back. "This is a Wills Wing Condor, it's huge and really works in this kind of light wind. This thing's very forgiving—it's only used for training."

We walked out through the lower sand hills to find a launch site that would fit the wind and our skill levels. Padraic and Michael were beginners as well, on vacation, thought they'd go for it. The takeoff point we picked was just below the crest of a dune. I could feel the wind coming up off the ocean. We set out two lines of small hot-pink flags to mark a flight path. Steve said, "We'll aim for those trees down where it levels off. You won't get that far, but your kite will go where you're looking—if you look down at the sand, that's where you'll end up."

You run downhill to take off, your hands holding the front crossbar. When the lift comes, you pull up your feet and your body hangs suspended by the harness, clipped into the rigging by a carabiner. I had talked my Irish friends into going first, as foreign guests; my crashing and laughing soon followed theirs. But Michael improved and Padraic even accomplished a standup landing one hundred feet away.

I can remember the feeling of my one good flight that day. The kite wanted to lift. I kept an easy touch on the bar and held my head up, keeping the distant trees in sight. Steve was running behind me, "Go! You got it!" For five seconds I was flying. I was lighter than the air and moving within it. It is a release that is both physical and emotional. In the moment before balance escaped, I thought, "*That's* it. That's why people want to keep doing this."

The lift is created by the wind, but also by the camber of the wing. Without lift, there can be no flight. The airfoil curvature directs a flow that is faster over the top surface, creating a lower pressure, allowing the wing to rise. In the Wrights' photographs, you can sense the lift of their '02 glider and imagine the smiles. In September and October they logged more than a thousand glides, expecting each time they launched to cruise out more than five hundred feet. They had a plane that was working, and time and place to fly it. Orville wrote about 1902, and flying close to a hundred times in a single day:

"Our runway was short, and it required a wind with a velocity of at least twelve miles an hour to lift the machine. I recall sitting in it, ready to cast off, one still day when the breeze seemed approaching. It came presently, rippling the daisies in the field, and just as it reached me I started the glider on the runway. But the innocent-appearing breeze was a whirlwind. It jerked the front of the machine sharply upward. I tilted my rudder to descend. Then the breeze spun downward, driving the glider to the ground with a tremendous shock and spinning me out head-first. That's just a sample of what we had to learn about air currents; nobody had ever heard of 'holes' in the air at that time." And later, describing their flights in a speech, Wilbur said, "If you are looking for perfect safety, you will do well to sit on a fence and watch the birds; but if you really wish to learn, you must mount a machine and become acquainted with its tricks by actual trial."

In October 2002, I return to the Outer Banks to watch real pros sailing off the dunes aboard a replica of the Wrights' '02 glider. It's a great morning to fly. The sky's bright and, after three days of calm, the wind is up. All along the Outer Banks the American and North Carolina flags are snapping straight out from their poles. I stop to pick up some coffee, load film in my camera, and drive to Jockey's Ridge State Park.

A Nags Head Fire and Rescue unit is backed up to the main

trail leading into the dunes. Red lights are flashing. I feel a twinge of fear that I recognize from my own few tries at hang gliding from Jockey's Ridge.

A stretcher is loaded and the ambulance pulls quietly away. I put on a wind jacket and start up the hill. The first person I see coming down says, "Somebody on the ground crew got whacked."

The accident—a back injury and not serious—happened to one of Nick Engler's employees from Dayton. Engler runs the Wright Brothers Aeroplane Company. He's written books on woodworking, and his admiration for the craftsmanship of Wilbur and Orville led him to try building working reproductions of all the planes, starting with the 1899 kite on through the 1905 flyer. When October comes, he likes to put a glider in a trailer and head down to North Carolina and the ninety-foot dune at Jockey's Ridge. He brought his 1900 model in 2000, the 1901 in 2001, and now the current edition, to honor the hundredth anniversary of the Wrights' '02 flying season.

Three highly skilled young military pilots are flying his glider today. For them, it's a fun assignment, fresh air and sun and the perplexity of trying to launch a thirty-two-foot-wide wood-and-cloth aircraft and hold altitude while skimming down the side of a sand dune. For Nick's company, it's a media win, plenty of reporters, a History Channel TV crew, and a video team shooting for the Defense Department. The pilots wear shorts, T-shirts, and sunglasses. From the navy, Lieutenant Commander Klas Ohman. The air force has sent Captain Jim Alexander. Captain Tanya Markow is here from the army, and usually flies the AH-64A Apache. As someone in the parking lot says, she's the "helicopter chick pilot." Jim Alexander pilots an

MC-130P Combat Shadow, and Klas Ohman flies an F/A-18C Hornet off the carrier USS *Kitty Hawk,* which operates from Yokosuka, Japan.

This day on the dunes the military pilots are in their learning curve, flying the '02 glider. The pilot climbs onto the lower wing, lying prone on a sliding cradle. A shift of the hips, to one side or the other, changes the banking angle of the wingtips. Both hands rest on a wooden control bar at chest level. The bar is linked to the small, wing-shaped elevator out in front of the pilot. If he wants the elevator, and therefore the glider, to pitch up, he rotates his wrists backward. Rolling the hands forward would cause the craft to pitch down.

Two launch crew members are at the end of each wing, one to help hold the craft at the proper angle, the other out in front with a rope to keep it from flipping over backwards. The pilot pushes up from the control bar, with elbows almost straight, and decides: "Ready. Go!" The launch crew runs down the slant of the dune, the pilot feels the onrushing wind, senses the moment of lift, waits a few more seconds, and yells, "Release!"

What follows is either a long, floating glide with an elegant landing, or a quick spinout as the plane follows one errant wingtip and scruffs and bangs into the sand.

By day's end, all the military pilots have a scrape or two, and will find bruises in the morning. The navy flyer, Klas Ohman, tells me, "There's a completely different set of motor skills here. Every plane we have flown has either a stick or a yoke. I've had a couple of stalls." I ask, "Does it feel like an airplane?" "Absolutely. And the first time it took off on me, it was really exciting." The army helicopter pilot, Tanya Markow, says, "All three of us have been trained in our aircraft. We had an instructor, and everyone who learns how to fly today has someone to teach them. The Wrights had to learn how to do it themselves. And when they crashed, they didn't know if it was their design or their flying. We know this plane flies, and so our mistakes belong to us."

My photographs taken on Jockey's Ridge that day remind me that I failed to make the acquaintance of two slim, well-dressed gentlemen who were watching the flights, smiling and talking with spectators and the pilots. They were local portrayers of Wilbur and Orville, wearing turn-of-the-last-century suits and wool caps. Wilbur clean-shaven, Orville with a mustache. If you wanted to make a movie, and had soft-focus lenses and old black-and-white film and the '02 reproduction and Jockey's Ridge on a windy day, and these two men . . .

The 1902 Wright brothers glider, after some modification, was a success. They were confident they could build a machine that would take off and travel under its own power; it was now a matter of finding an engine that was weight-effective and a propeller that would work in air as opposed to water. But just a year earlier they'd seemed ready to quit. The 1901 model hadn't produced the lift they needed or expected. They left the Outer Banks in late August after weeks of erratic flying and discouraging rain. On the train home to Ohio, Wilbur talked with his brother, recalling later, "When we looked at the time and money which we had expended and considered the progress made and the distance yet to go, we considered our experiments a failure. At this time I made the prediction that man would sometime fly but that it would not be within our lifetime."

✢   ✢

They returned to the bicycle business, which their repairman and machinist Charlie Taylor had been running, and kept trying to puzzle through the disappointing performance of the 1901 glider. In their designs the brothers had been using data gathered with experiments and instruments by Otto Lilienthal for his flights in Germany, but now the figures seemed wrong. In September Wilbur went to Chicago to give a speech to the Western Society of Engineers. He described the North Carolina test flights, showed magic lantern slides of the glider—and dared to suggest that the Lilienthal tables might be in error.

Back in their Dayton bike shop, Wilbur and his brother soon solved the puzzle, using trigonometry, scraps of metal, bits of bicycle spokes, and a motor-driven fan to generate wind. They crafted a six-foot-long wooden tunnel, with a glass section in the top for viewing; the airflow inside was about thirty miles an hour. Then they fashioned all sorts of tiny wing shapes, mounting them at differing angles on delicate balance instruments in order to calculate their efficiency. They could measure lift—the *upward* force produced by the airstream, and drag, the force *generated* by the wing. The brothers kept meticulous records, and at the end of the wind tunnel sessions they had a large array of lift and drag coefficients from which to design their wings.

For the earlier gliders the Wrights had used the Smeaton air density coefficient as part of the equation for predicting lift. John Smeaton was a British civil engineer who had a special interest in fluid mechanics—waterwheels and windmills. What became known as the Smeaton coefficient for the pressure of wind on a surface derives from his work, and for more than a century everyone, including Lilienthal, and now the Wrights, had used the Smeaton number of .0055 as a multiplier in the equation. After the tunnel experiments the Wrights could rely on their own data to assess lift, but Wilbur had already concluded than the Smeaton coefficient was off. He looked at notes from some of the previous summer's flying and calculated that .0055 was too high. "I see no good reason for using a greater coefficient than .0033," he wrote. Their 1901 glider, it was now apparent, had been designed to underperform.

From my reading, I could have only a vague sense of what all this meant in the business of airfoil design. I knew a real conversation would help, and went to see Ken Hyde, an aircraft builder who's spent a great deal of time working through the difficulties the Wrights faced with the lift and drag numbers. Hyde, in his workshop at his home outside Warrenton, Virginia, told me, "Wilbur and Orville had it right. About .0033. That's the true number. That's what the Wrights got in 1901 with reverse math and practical application, and that's what we build airplanes to today. It's .0033 plus a lot of other numbers on out to the right. You remember Octave Chanute wrote to them and said don't be so cocksure that someone isn't going to fly before you do, but they *were* cocksure. Nobody had this number, nobody understood it, and they had given Chanute the tables and explained how it worked, but these guys were not members of the academic community so they couldn't possibly know what the hell they were talking about. *Nobody* really got it until they saw Wilbur fly in France in 1908."

Ken Hyde is slight, with brown hair and a cautious gaze. People say descriptions of Wilbur Wright would work as well for Hyde. He's a retired American Airlines pilot —thirty-three years of service. When he was still in high school he worked as an apprentice mechanic, trading job hours for flying lessons, and he's always had a sideline aircraft restoration business.

Ken Hyde has built flying reproductions of all three Wright gliders: the 1900, the '01, and the '02. Now his Wright Experience team is finishing a 1903 powered machine. This will be the plane that attempts flight at Kill Devil Hills at 10:35 on the morning of December 17, 2003. He has authorization from the National Park Service, and considerable corporate support.

The Wright Experience workshop is a spacious pale-khaki metal building down a gravel drive past Ken's house and a pond. It's farm and horse country, with low hills. You can sometimes see the Blue Ridge Mountains to the west and, often, a 747 drifting into Dulles Airport to the northeast. There's a two-thousand-foot grass runway between the workshop and the tree line, and it's handy for glider training. I've seen video shot from the pilot's perspective: A tow rope is secured to the back of a car, which pulls the craft along until it lifts off and gains enough altitude to call it flying. One could imagine that when his team is satisfied with their work on the '03 machine, they will bring it out to this grass strip, start the motor, take some pictures. In late fall they'll truck the plane to the Outer Banks and wait for a perfect day to fly a test. If it happens, Ken hopes, there will not be a word of that moment in the newspapers.

Ken Hyde shows me the airy wood skeleton of the '03, the wing assemblies of ash ribs—120 total—that have been cut and soaked and steamed and bent into their curves, waiting to be covered with fabric. It is admirable workmanship. Ken says, "The tools of the early 1900s for doing things by hand were far better than we've got today. Sharper ripsaws and gouges. It takes someone who's got some use in his fingers to do what they did. They even made their own taps and dies."

Indeed, after failing to find an engine maker that would build to the brothers' specifications, Orville took on the job himself, with Charlie Taylor's expert help. They had a foundry cast the aluminum block, and Charlie fashioned the steel crank. The first aircraft engine produced twelve horsepower.

Ken's shop has a full array of hand tools and heavy-duty machinery ("I gave my wife that Bridgeport milling machine for Christmas"), encouraging a departure from contemporary airplane construction: "If we need a special piece of tubing, you call the tubing company and they say we don't have any of that but we can make it and it's going to cost you a hundred thousand dollars and we have to run at least fifty thousand feet of it and what's coming through the telephone is that they don't want to be bothered, so you wake up one morning and come down and get a piece of one-inch tubing and a piece of three-quarter-inch square stock and you put it in a vise and tighten it down and *wham* it comes out to the exact dimensions. The biggest problem with all the work we're doing here is getting back to the simplicity of what the Wrights did."

The prop shop is next. Using wind-tunnel data, the Wrights built their own propellers, because they quickly realized that designs intended for boats were useless out of the water. Ken says, "This is probably their biggest discovery and the thing they've been given the least credit for. They were the first people to determine that the propeller is actually a wing in rotation. It had to be the hardest thing they undertook, making those. We tried to find a prop company that would carve them for us, but the old-timers who knew how to do it were gone or too old.

And the company flat refused to make a prop from spruce because it's not very strong. They wanted to use yellow birch with five or six laminations and the props would have weighed thirty-five pounds. So we do it ourselves; our guys, Larry Parks and Dave Meyer, use a spokeshave and a drawknife and make a six-pound propeller."

Ken Hyde has been gathering Wright relics over the years, from complete engines to a shard of wood from a wing frame. In an upstairs office he gently unwraps a folding of yellowed fabric. It measures four feet across. In 1903 it covered part of the left lower wing of the Wright Flyer. The fabric is on loan from Marianne Miller Hudec, Wilbur and Orville's grandniece.

"This is Pride of the West muslin. You can see the watermarks from the Dayton flood of 1913. See the nail holes where it was put on the spar? Half-inch nails, lots of them. This is like the Shroud of Turin for us because you can see where the metal fittings rubbed through, so we can set the spacing of the ribs. We've had this analyzed by the McCrone laboratory in Illinois—they actually did the work on the Shroud of Turin—and they gave us the thread count and checked everything including these spots. Somebody asked if that was Orville's blood, and it turned out to be iron oxide from a leaking old tin roof."

The fabric is close to me on the table. Ken may be wondering if I would dare touch it. I do.

A few months later I drive to Langley Air Force Base to watch the 2003 version of Pride of the West muslin rippling in the breeze. Ken Hyde's Flyer is poised on the test platform of a wind tunnel that is so big I feel like I'm in an IMAX movie.

My vantage point is a walkway at the side of the platform, and slightly below. I'm looking up at the '03 machine, now finished, although today it's missing the engine and propellers. The plane stands high atop an array of blue steel struts and appears to be flying. In theoretical fact it is: two huge fans are pulling air over the wings, past the rudder and the front elevator, at twenty-five miles an hour. It is fifty-eight degrees in the unheated tunnel, and the wind chill forces me to wear a down coat and hat and gloves. The conditions are close to what Wilbur and Orville faced on December 17, 1903.

The Langley Full Scale Tunnel is part of the NASA complex at Langley Air Force Base in Hampton, Virginia, and dates back to 1931. Francis Rogallo, the hang-gliding visionary, was the wind-tunnel manager in the mid-1940s. NASA now has several far more sophisticated tunnels on site, and in 1997 it turned this older one over to Old Dominion University. The LFST is an attraction for engineering students, and the school runs the tunnel as a break-even business. The Wright Flyer testing is a donation by the school; the usual fee is $10,000 a day. Rubbermaid wants to know how well its garden sheds stand up to wind? They test them here. Road signs are checked for wind-load. Volvo tractor-trailer trucks have been on the platform. But NASCAR racing teams are the best customers. Drew Landman, the tunnel's chief engineer, says, "We've had about fifty NASCAR crews bring cars here. It seems like a mystical science to them, but I think they get something out of it, little tweaks that could make a big difference when you're going around a track at 180."

I ask, "Can you give them any ideas?"

"As an engineer you have to remain neutral. You can't transfer the technology. I've just got to sit there and make sure they get the data in the best possible format. I can't say, 'You guys are messing up big-time.'"

The race cars sit on the platform where the Gemini space capsule was tested. All the World War II fighter planes were checked out here. In a hallway there's a 1934 group photograph, taken outside the tunnel building—Orville Wright is at the center of the first row. And now the ghost of his plane is here. Under the lights, the ruffling fabric takes on a golden, ethereal look.

"Looks like it wants to go, doesn't it?" asks Bill Hadden, a mechanic on Ken Hyde's crew. He's been here for the plane's setup, the rigging of sensors, the slow lift by overhead crane to the center of the test stand, the attachment to the struts, which control the plane's angle and transmit load information.

Bill says, "It's a little tense, here with this plane. They turn the airflow up, and you're not sure at first if something might crack, or what if something flew off and hit one of those fan blades— you'd be talking about a million dollars. They have raccoons in this tunnel, and one morning we came in and found footprints on the wing covering. Ken doesn't even want people to touch this fabric without gloves. And to hear that there were raccoon tracks? Plus some stains from water leaking from the roof of the truck we brought it down in? Ken flew a fabric conservator in and she figured out how to treat the stains and plump up the little raccoon-print depressions."

Bill and I sit in the back of the control room, watching the engineers watch the gauges and TV monitors as the test gets under way. Some of the men are gray and balding, wearing plaid shirts, some are graduate students in sweatshirts and jeans.

Bill says, "The retired NASA techs like to come volunteer on this project. Last night I went to dinner with a guy who made the sensor package we're using to track the warp of the wingtips on our '03 plane. It's really sophisticated computer stuff and he just walked in and said, 'You might think of using something like this.'"

At the test console, the talk is quietly measured. The goal is to find out if this plane could have flown in the winds of December 17, and to collect data for an '03 flight simulator.

You will hear an engineer say, "Another click of Q," or one more mile per hour in speed ("Q" is simply a letter assigned to stand for the dynamic pressure of the wind). Then, "He's trying to get a load factor of 1 for various angles of attack." Then, "Four hundred pounds of lift here and to go to 750 means doubling the Q and I don't think I want to go there, not on my watch." And, "It doesn't make sense, Q is Q."

The test runs are about twenty minutes. As one is ending, I go out into the echoing space and watch the plane's fabric smooth as the two fans—propellers, really, with four spruce blades and a thirty-six-foot diameter—slow and then hold stationary.

But the test isn't over until "wind stop." I've heard them call out that point in the control room. The airflow is continuous past the plane and the fans and then in channels around the building to enter again behind the platform. It takes a few minutes for such a volume of air to quiet down. I know the engineers are watching a monitor, and have zoomed in on a railing in front of the fans. A small piece of white yarn is tied there, and when it's no longer moving the test run is over.

A fluttering length of string was the first flight instrument. The Wrights used it as an attitude indicator, to show whether the plane was pitching up or down or banking. A modern sailplane pilot still uses string, for precisely the same reason.

CHAPTER FOUR

HUFFMAN PRAIRIE

IN THE DIFFUSE LIGHT OF A CLOUDY OHIO MORNING THE blossoms and birds are jewels: tiny goldfinches, purple coneflowers and thistles. Black-and-white bobolinks, trilling, fly over yellow oxeye; two white moths, in twinned darting movements, arrive to settle on the ivory sprays of Queen Anne's lace. I can hear bees circling, and cicadas, even the grass in motion with the wind.

A darker sound starts to the north, and becomes the takeoff roar of a C-141 Starlifter, curving up out of Wright-Patterson Air Force Base on four plumes of exhaust. The plane is off the runway before it passes, and is quickly gone over the southeast horizon. Terri Lucas, a biologist at the base, watches with me and says, "I grew up around here and the kids would say that the rabbits were deaf—they'd all lost their hearing because of the planes. I also used to hear about the little green men the government had stored at Wright-Pat. The planes were really bad back then. The

Strategic Air Command was flying all the time. I was afraid of Martians and when I'd hear those planes I would hide."

Wright-Patterson AFB is named for Wilbur and Orville, and in honor of Lieutenant Frank Stuart Patterson, who was killed here in a 1918 crash when the army was testing the synchronization of a machine gun with a propeller. What is now a military vastness on the edge of Dayton had its beginnings as the Huffman Prairie Flying Field. Once these rough mowed paths through the tall grasses *were* the runways.

On several days in late summer I went out to Wright-Pat to wander around the black-dirt prairie in the floodplain of the nearby Mad River. Orville has left us a sketch of the flying field, as he and his brother and their mechanic, Charlie Taylor, laid it out in 1904 after they had cut the grass with scythes. It's an oval, set well inside the triangle of pasture they borrowed from Torrence Huffman, a Dayton bank president. If you bring along some old photographs, as I did, you'll recognize the line of trees on the near side of the country road at the field's western boundary. The flying was done counterclockwise. They'd take off into a west wind and then bank south. A single honey locust— a large, thorny tree—stood as a threat at the far end of the oval, and marked their turning point. The only structure on the field was a wooden hangar. The Wrights rebuilt it twice over the years, and archaeologists have used airborne thermal sensing and ground-penetrating radar to determine precisely where the last one stood. Thousands of artifact bits have been found there— glass and wire, bolts, turnbuckles, links of drive chain.

Wilbur and Orville, after their four flights at Kitty Hawk on December 17, 1903, crated up their aircraft and engine and tools and made their way—by boat and train—back home for Christmas with their father Milton, Katharine, and brother Lorin and his family. They must have laughed when they saw the hometown newspapers. A headline on the front page of the *Dayton Evening Herald* declared, PROBLEM OF AERIAL NAVIGATION SOLVED, above a story that had Wilbur at the controls for a speedy three-mile flight into the "teeth of a gale." The *Dayton Daily News* wrote about the WRIGHT FLYER: CLEVER DEVICE OF BISHOP WRIGHT'S SONS, REMARKABLE ACHIEVEMENT OF TWO OF DAYTON'S INDUSTRIOUS YOUNG MEN. This story, while more accurate, ran inside the paper, on page twelve.

But the brothers had flown, had a photograph to prove it, and they had a new craft in mind: sturdier, more powerful, and one that would be protected by worldwide legal patents. They lived in a house their father owned and their sister took care of. They had several thousand dollars in savings and loan accounts. They had a bicycle business that paid them a living, kept tools close at hand and was slow in the winter months. They would build a Wright Flyer II.

It was early spring of 1904 when Orville and Wilbur, thinking about a new flying field, got on a streetcar that took them from the West Side across the bridge over the Great Miami River, into downtown Dayton. From there it was a fast ride on the Dayton, Springfield & Urbana Interurban Railway, eight miles to the northeast and the country crossroads stop known as Simms Station. Orville knew about Huffman Prairie because he had been here on one of his high school botany field trips. In the archives of Wright State University, nearby, you can see his 1887 notebook with graceful pencil sketches of leaves and buds, and lists of observed springtime flowers—skunk cabbage, larkspur, marsh marigold, wild verbena.

The brothers walked the pasture, estimating the flying space, watching for a breeze. There would be enough room, just. The site was somewhat secluded, with a few farmhouses around. It was easy to get back and forth on the trolley, running every hour. It wasn't North Carolina—wide-open and windy—but it was home. They decided to go see Mr. Huffman at the Fourth National Bank. He said they could use the land without charge, but they had to be careful about the livestock, a problem Wilbur mentioned in a letter.

"In addition to cattle there have been a dozen or more horses in the pasture and as it is surrounded by barbwire fencing we have been at much trouble to get them safely away before making trials. Also the ground is an old swamp and is filled with grassy hummocks some six inches high so that it resembles a prairie-dog town. This makes the track laying slow work. While we are getting ready the favorable opportunities slip away, and we are usually up against a rainstorm, a dead calm, or a wind blowing at right angles to the track." The launch track system was the same as devised on the Outer Banks. Long sections of two-by-four lumber were placed end to end, held on edge by stakes. The airplane rode along the track balanced on a dolly attached to a bicycle hub. As Wilbur's note suggests, the takeoff would ideally be directly into the wind, and if that shifted, so must the track.

By late May the brothers had cleared a field, built a sturdy wooden hangar, but their newly designed plane didn't want to fly. They had trouble even matching the distance numbers from the previous year's Kitty Hawk flights. If the Flyer II rose at all, it would struggle to get past a hundred feet. The winds in Ohio were certainly lighter, but Harry Combs, a veteran pilot and author, believes that the "density altitude" at Huffman Prairie was the main problem. At Kitty Hawk, December 17, the temperature was thirty-four degrees, the air was dry, and they were at sea level. "In effect," he writes, "the air was thick, and gave all the airfoils that bit into it—the propellers as well as the wings—much more efficiency. These were prime flying conditions." Huffman Prairie, 815 feet above sea level, on a day in May 1904, had air that was hot and humid. Combs concludes: "The Wrights had an aircraft of marginal performance at best; to get into the air it needed everything it had. Between the two sets of conditions present at Kitty Hawk and Simms Station, there was a density altitude differential of about 4,700 feet!"

Earlier in 1904 the Wrights thought they might be ready for an aeronautical competition in the fall. The St. Louis World's Fair, which would open a year behind schedule, was to commemorate the 1803 Louisiana Purchase, and had attracted the attention of aviators from all over the world with the promise of a $100,000 prize for the best flight. Wilbur and Orville went to St. Louis to look over the site, but later, perhaps discouraged by the Flyer II's early performance, decided to save the $250 entry fee and stay home. As it turned out, there was no heavier-than-air flying in St. Louis, only balloons and airships. The event itself was a financial failure without any prize money to award, but for several years the World's Fair had served as a beacon in the dreams of aviators. Wilbur wrote to Octave Chanute: "The newspapers are full of accounts of flying machines which have been building in cellars, garrets, stables and other secret places, each one of which will undoubtedly carry off the hundred

thousand dollars at St. Louis." He may have read about the
Ezekiel Airship Company in Texas. A Baptist minister, biblically
inspired, said he had built a winged machine that was guided
and powered by "a wheel within a wheel," and that it flew one
Sunday morning in 1902. The Reverend Burrell Cannon,
broke, departed the town of Pittsburg, Texas, with his airship on
a railroad flatcar, headed for the St. Louis World's Fair and the
first prize. A storm blew the Ezekiel Airship off the train, and,
it is said, Reverend Cannon left the pieces on the ground.

At Huffman Prairie, in early September 1904, the prospects
seemed better for the Flyer II as the Wrights solved the problem
of takeoff acceleration. They devised a derrick that would
launch their aircraft, much in the same way a modern jet fighter
is propelled from the deck of an aircraft carrier.

Wilbur and Orville built a metal tower twenty feet high,
coming to a peak at the top like a teepee. A pulley system raised
1,600 pounds of lead weights. A rope ran from the top of the
tower, down under the rail to the front, and then back up along
the top to connect with the plane. One brother and Charlie
Taylor, and perhaps some friends or passersby, helped haul on
the rope to lift the weights. The other brother, prone in the
pilot's position on the lower wing, gave a signal and the weights
fell and catapulted the plane along the track and into the air.

Charlie Webbert of Dayton volunteered for a day's rope duty,
and told a reporter:

"Well, sir, we pulled that fool thing around over the ground
of Huffman Prairie about thirty or forty times, hoisting it up on
the derrick so it would get a good start, and we were all hot and
sweaty and about played out. What was the use of our wasting

our time over such a ridiculous thing any longer? But once more we pulled her up again and let her go. The old engine seemed to be working a little better than normal. Orville stuck his head and nodded to Wilbur and Wilbur turned her loose. *And by God the damn thing flew.*"

As fall approached, the air cooled and cleared and the flights got longer. Then turning the aircraft became a challenge, as the distance down one side of the oval course was not even a thousand feet. They were always about to make a turn or thinking about it. Wilbur said, "At first we did not know just how much movement to give in order to make a circle of a given size. On the first three trials we found that we had started a circle on too large a radius to keep within the boundaries of the small field in which we were operating. Accordingly, a landing was made each time, without accident, merely to avoid passing the boundaries of the field."

Enter A. I. Root, owner of the A. I. Root Company, a leading supplier of beekeeping equipment, and publisher of the journal *Gleanings in Bee Culture*. Amos Root loved to follow technology, and he liked conveyances: He'd imported a French velocipede, a bicycle that he'd read about in *Scientific American,* and was an early, enthusiastic automobile owner.

At his home in Medina, Ohio, Root was hearing accounts of an airplane flying first in North Carolina and now above farm fields near Dayton. With the blessing of the Wrights, he made the trip in September 1904, driving two hundred miles down across Ohio from Medina. He took a room with a farm family across the road from Huffman Prairie, met Wilbur and Orville, and watched them fly.

Root made a promise not to print anything until the Wrights gave permission, but did publish this, deep inside the *Gleanings* October issue: "We want a machine that will float as easily and as safely as the bees, the butterflies, and the carrier pigeons. May the Lord be praised, this is already in sight."

Finally, in January, Amos Root told his readers what he had seen at Huffman Prairie, as Wilbur took the fourth flight on a cloudy, wet afternoon. It was the first published eyewitness account of a Wright brothers flight:

It was my privilege, on the 20th day of September, 1904 to see the first successful trip of an airship, without a balloon to sustain it, that the world has ever made, that is, to turn the corners and come back to the starting point. . . . The engine is started and got up to speed. The machine is held until ready to start by a sort of trap to be sprung when all is ready; then with a tremendous flapping and snapping of the four-cylinder engine, the huge machine springs aloft. When it first turned that circle and came near the starting point, I was right in front of it; and I said then, and I believe still, it was one of the grandest sights, if not the grandest sight of my life. Imagine a locomotive that has left its track, and is climbing up in the air right toward you—a locomotive without any wheels, we will say, but with white wings instead. . . . Well, now imagine this white locomotive, with wings that spread 20 feet each way, coming right toward you with a tremendous flap of its propellers, and you will have something like what I saw. The younger brother bade me move to one side for fear it might come down suddenly. . . . These two brothers have probably not even a fair glimpse of what their discovery is going to bring to the children of men.

✛ ✛

Amos Root had seen the best of the 1904 season, indeed the best of the Wrights' flying to date. The next month brought a series of accidents, breaking propellers and wing struts. Then Wilbur managed a five-minute flight, circling the field four times, and Orville matched it on December 1, before the Flyer II was dismantled.

Over the winter, in the back of the Wrights' bicycle shop, the 1905 Flyer took shape. It was more graceful in appearance, and, it was hoped, more stable in the air. The '04 model often refused to come out of a turn, so the brothers decided to add a separate lever for the vertical rudder, at the rear. Now there were three controls: With the front elevator they could move the nose up or down (pitch). A push or pull of the wing-warping lever would cause the plane to bank into a turn (roll), and a change in the rudder angle would affect the side-to-side attitude (yaw). This was the first airplane to be independently controlled in all three elements of flight, and it would require some pilot training. The adjustments, the experiments, continued through a rainy summer, at Huffman Prairie and late at night in the bike shop. The elevator was made larger and extended farther out in front. The rudder gained more square footage. The propellers were redesigned. In October, Orville flew seventeen minutes before a rear bearing overheated. He flew thirty-three minutes until a transmission bearing failed. Later, Wilbur set off on a flight that lasted thirty-eight minutes and covered almost twenty-five miles, coming down when the gasoline tank was dry.

The Wright brothers, at the end of 1905, had finished the airplane they had set out to build. They could swoop into turns, they could fly a figure-eight, they could sustain long, circling flights—and the potential of the 1905 Flyer seemed limitless. Now it was time to move from airplane design to airplane business. The U.S. War Department seemed skeptical that the Wrights really had such a plane and wanted to see drawings. The brothers, guarding their patent potential, refused. The British appeared interested, and the French. Demonstration flights would have helped, but the brothers decided not to fly until a contract was signed—it became a matter of honor. Before the Wrights returned to the air, 1906 would go by, and 1907 as well.

Huffman Prairie was a flight training field, off and on, until the end of World War II. Then it lay quiet, only a small section of Wright-Patterson's open grasslands, saved from development because of its legacy and a tendency to stay wet. It was kept mowed and occasionally used as a parachute drop zone.

In 1988, Dave Nolin, a Wright State biology graduate student, rediscovered the prairie. He noticed the Huffman site on an old surveyor's map, and persuaded his father, a Wright-Pat civil service employee, to take him onto the base, where, by coincidence, the mowing crews were behind schedule and the prairie grasses were waving tall in the wind and going to seed.

Nolin called Terri Lucas, and that's how she now gets to manage Ohio's largest tallgrass prairie remnant as well as Wright-Pat's hunting and fishing programs. Volunteers come often to help dig out the thistles and woody growths of hawthorn, Russian olive, and silver maple. In the fall, the fire department comes by to set a controlled burn.

Terri points out the boundaries of the site, as we walk a pathway through the shoulder-high big bluestem and Indian grass. "It's a hundred and nine acres. I just took the chunk that had the best of the prairie on it and expanded it as far as I could go either way. The air force has been good about it. I saw a drawing once where they wanted to take part of the prairie to park airplanes that had explosives on board, and legally they could have done it."

In the evening, when the visitors have left, the Indiana bats come out from the tree line, forty or so strong, hunting for insects. That's also Eric Metzler's work. "Have you talked with the moth guy?" people kept asking me. So I looked him up.

Metzler is a freelance entomologist who drives in for night visits from his home in Columbus, Ohio. He makes surveys, listing what sorts of lepidoptera—butterflies and moths—inhabit Huffman Prairie.

Early one morning I helped him carry his traps out of the prairie, back to his truck. The insects are collected overnight, attracted by a battery-powered blue fluorescent tube.

"Why do the insects like this light?" I asked.

"Nobody knows," Metzler said. "What it looks like to a bug's eye, I haven't a clue."

The collectors have a garbage can lid on top, and a funnel in the bottom section, which is a five-gallon plastic bucket, to let the rain run out.

We dismantled the traps and laid the parts out on the pavement. Metzler started dumping the insects into plastic trays. Most were dead, some twitching. It was suddenly very hot. "What is the poison?"

Metzler said, "The poison is cyanide, and most people can't get cyanide and probably shouldn't have it, but it's available to those of us who do this for a living. What I do is build a small gas chamber—with cyanide granules in these cloth bags. It kills the insects very rapidly and doesn't make them real stiff."

A cautionary odor rose from the traps. "Burnt almond is what cyanide smells like. It's okay if you breathe it ambiently."

In a tray were two inches of insects and dusty wing parts and a litter of small, green leafhoppers. Metzler plucked out a pure white moth. "*Haploa reversa*—this one tastes bad to birds. Here's one, a tiger moth that will make bats vomit. The caterpillar of this sphinx moth has a real startling horn on its back, but it's perfectly harmless."

"Like the one in *The Silence of the Lambs?*" I asked.

"Yes."

Metzler guessed we had five to six hundred moths in our tray, just from the one trap. Of those there might be close to a hundred species, and possibly the moth that he discovered in 1994, and thereby earned the honor of naming. "I called it *Glyphidocera wrightorum*. It means 'of the Wrights.' It's a very tiny moth, maybe a quarter of an inch wide, and it'll take my microscope at home to find it." Another species now to Metzler's credit is *Gnorimoschema huffmanellum*—"comes from Huffman."

"I can't show you those, but look here." He finds a moth with a parchment look to the wings. "If you do this"—and he pulled open the wings, two on each side, standing at right angles to the body—"if you pull these out, this moth resembles the Wright Flyer." And on the upturned bottom of his thumb he balanced another specimen, tiny and brown, with backswept wings. "Pterophoridae. A lot of name for such a little moth, but this one, see, this one looks like a jet airplane ready to take off."

✛　✛

I walk twice around the Huffman Prairie oval, rushing along looking up, trying to coax a spirit from the sky. I want to *duck* as the white biplane dips overhead, a wingtip close to the ground in the curve around the thorn tree, and to *feel* the banging of Charlie Taylor's unmuffled four-cylinder engine. But I am left with only a legacy of those days—the distant whoosh of a C-141 landing on a Wright-Pat runway.

The clouds would have been the same, though, a hundred years ago. I've been watching them gather in the late afternoons, and it's a real Midwestern sky this far out in Ohio, with an extravagance of airspace. Here at their flying field, Wilbur and Orville, and maybe Charlie, would have sat on the edge of the hangar floor, waiting to hear the trolley car coming along from Springfield. The day would have cooled off. They would hang around and talk and joke a bit about the day's flights, and watch the sky. The huge white clouds would float in from the west and stack up in towers. Either brother could name the clouds, and knew well the terms introduced in London in 1802 by the thirty-year-old chemist and amateur meteorologist Luke Howard: *cumulus* (pile or heap), *cirrus* (fiber or hair), and *stratus* (meaning layer, sheet). All the names came from Latin; Howard also used *nimbus* when he wanted to add rain to a cloud's description.

In a war just a decade away, a young pilot with a fast and strong plane would marvel at the experience of entering the world above the highest clouds. Cecil Lewis wrote in his memoir, *Sagittarius Rising*:

> Mist wraiths drew back and showed blue. I put the
> machine level and gazed about in wonder. As far as

the eye could reach, to the four horizons, a level plain of radiant whiteness, sparkling in the sun. The light seemed not to come from a single source, but to pervade and permeate every atom of air—a dazzling, perfect empty basin of blue. We moved like spirits in an airy loom, where wind and cloud and light wove day and night long the endless fabric of the changing sky.

Did the Wrights ever imagine climbing twenty, thirty thousand feet in the air to reach the top layers of a cloud formation? Possibly. But it was difficult in 1904 and 1905, with a tiny, troublesome aircraft, thirty feet off the ground, to think of traveling very far. At Huffman Prairie, early on, they stayed within their eighty-five-acre limits, not confident about their right to fly over anyone else's property, and perhaps worried how to get the plane home if they did land miles away.

CHAPTER FIVE

ABOVE FRANCE

THE WHITE AIRPORT VAN SEEMS TO FLOAT THROUGH THE empty streets of Paris, early on a Sunday morning. The driver is singing softly with the music. It's an aria—a soprano voice.

"What is this we're listening to?" I lean forward and make a rolling motion with my hand.

He pauses the dashboard CD player to take out the disc.

"Sumi Jo," he shows me. "Korean."

It's a *bel canto* collection, and music from Bellini's *La Sonnambula* accompanies our arrival at the hotel. The driver smiles—a touch of opera helps clear the confusion of an all-night flight and deserves a gracious tip.

I had arrived from Washington Dulles on a United Boeing 777. As we landed at Charles de Gaulle, our pilot pointed out the supersonic Concorde, poised on a taxiway against a backdrop of Thai and Singapore Air 747s. Air cargo planes were arriving, charter flights taking off. My reasons for traveling to Paris have to do with how all this got started.

Wilbur Wright came to France in the spring of 1907 to sell airplanes. In the summer of 1908 he returned as a pilot, staying on through March of 1909. His flights—bringing the art of aviation together with its science—startled the French and amazed the world.

Wilbur's first trip across the ocean was on the RMS *Campania,* a Cunard steamship. The transatlantic liners could make five hundred miles a day, and it was a simple journey from Dayton: take the train to New York, get a night's sleep, sail in the morning for Liverpool. Even if you stopped off in London, you could be in France nine days later. Wilbur had a $250 cabin to himself for the crossing, paying only $100, he said, because the ship was just half full.

On his arrival, on crisp Hotel Meurice stationery, he wrote to Katharine back home: "We reached Paris about six this evening and are located on the Rue de Rivoli across the street from the Louvre gardens. The column Vendome is behind me, and the Place de la Concorde and the Arc de Triomphe are farther up the Champs Elysees. We are right in the most beautiful and interesting part of the city."

I have come to Paris in May, as Wilbur did. I have a fifth-floor room in the far more modest hotel next door to the Meurice. I open the lace curtains and tall windows to the same welcoming view—the Louvre to the left, the east; then the green expanse of the Jardin des Tuileries.

Wilbur did not mention the Eiffel Tower in describing this view to his sister, but at almost a thousand feet high it was already an aviator's landmark: in 1901 Alberto Santos-Dumont, in his powered, steerable balloon, completed a seven-mile course that circled the Eiffel Tower, winning a cash prize and becoming *Le Conquérant de l'Air*. Santos-Dumont, born in Brazil to family wealth, found joy in the skies over Paris—he would throw his brightly colored neckties down to the crowds. By the fall of 1906 he'd built an airplane: it had an engine, it had wings, and it rose from the grass and stayed aloft for twenty-one seconds. As the world saw it, he was flying.

A year before Santos-Dumont's brief venture, Wilbur had circled for twenty-five *miles* at Huffman Prairie, but his flight lacked official witness and was discounted by the Aero-Club de France, and by the highly competitive French people, who believed their country to be foremost in aviation. The Wrights had become known as *"les bluffeurs."* Despite this, Wilbur's intention in 1907 was to sell airplanes to the French Ministry of War. He was prepared to have a plane shipped over, but it would be the summer of 1908 before he flew.

After a short nap, I go out for a walk in the Tuileries. The day has become warm, and the clear light feels restorative. Young men are playing soccer, couples are close together on the green metal benches. Wilbur also walked along these sandy gravel paths, and described it for his father.

"The gardens of the Tuileries and Louvre are thronged with thousands of people who use it as a public playground. The children have their marbles & hoops and an interesting spool which they keep from falling off a string by keeping it revolving."

Here in the Tuileries, I find the same flower that I have in my own backyard in Maryland—a lovely orange blossom, a wildflower, I've thought. I ask several people nearby, *"Nom fleur?"* They all shake their heads, and then a woman, laughing, takes my notebook and writes *giroflée*. And next to it I put down *"jheeroh-flay."*

Though they are long gone today, there were still chestnut trees in America in Wilbur's time, but now, especially in spring, the chestnuts in the Tuileries are a wonder, with drapy, three-part leaves and creamy flowers.

Wilbur would have been watching the wind in these trees. He would have seen the toy sailboats in the breeze across the Tuileries' octagonal pond, and the blue, white, and red banner atop the nearby Grand Palais, indicating a fair wind aloft from the southeast. And he would have recalled reading about the 1783 excitement in the Tuileries when Jacques Charles and Marie-Noël Robert lifted off in a gondola underneath a small balloon filled with hydrogen gas. They had a barometer for measuring altitude; they had ballast they could throw overboard. They rose into the wind and soon heard a boom from a distant cannon, the agreed-upon signal from the Tuileries that the balloon was out of sight.

In July of his first summer in France, Wilbur Wright, again writing to his father, described his own lighter-than-air adventure:

> Yesterday I took a balloon trip with Mr. Hawley, Mr. Levee, and Mr. Harrington. We started from the Aero-Club grounds just across the river from the Bois de Boulogne about half past four in the afternoon. We at once arose to a height of about 2000 feet and sailed off to the southwest. At this height the irregularities of the ground are scarcely to be detected, that is the hills and val-

leys. On the other hand the different fields with their various colored crops are more brilliant than painting . . . we let [the balloon] rise into the clouds where we were in a dense fog through which we could see only a few feet. . . . we emerged from this fog into the brightest possible sunshine with a wonderfully blue sky. The clouds lay just below us resembling a hilly or mountainous country covered entirely with snow. The shadow of the balloon was thrown on the cloud banks and was surrounded by a halo which was very beautiful. After an hour of this we dropped below the clouds and again caught sight of the earth. We were miles from Paris in a very rich level country almost free from trees. Some times we would float along only a hundred feet from the ground with the guide trailing like a great snake behind us. . . . As our course would take us farther from a railroad if [we] went on, we dropped down into a wheat-field and ripped open the balloon with a rip cord. Though we were moving about 25 miles an hour we made a very nice landing, the grain acting as a cushion and brake. After packing the balloon we secured a cart and went to a little village about a mile away, and got some supper.

Wilbur's letter to the bishop is carefully written, with corrected phrases and added words, and unusually lyrical. His more characteristic July 17 diary entry notes the story without adjectives, and the following winter he published a gruff summation in *Scientific American,* as he compared balloons to airplanes:

"In ballooning, a few glorious hours in the air are usually followed by a tiresome walk to some village, an uncomfortable night at a poor hotel, and a return home by slow local trains."

He wrote in a different style for each member of his family.
With his sister, Katharine, he often was teasing, but also schol-
arly, with references to literature and art. In letters to his
younger brother Orville, he'd be friendly but tough—they were
business partners:

> MONDAY, PARIS, JUNE 23RD
>
> Dear Orville,
> I enclose copy of a proposition we intend
> to make to the French Minister of War.
> Unless they show indication of acceptance
> promptly, without substantial modification,
> we will not waste further time in France,
> but will go to Berlin.
>
> *Will*

Cablegram code was used for much of their communication.
Western Union provided business codes for its customers, as did
Charles Flint & Company, the Wrights' New York–based sales
agent, and no doubt the brothers made up some of their own,
for even more privacy.

> To: Wright, Hartoberg, Paris.

DOFINT ABSAME CRIMIN AMBALADI CHYLEM
DIRHEMFLIN

> (Do you not think it advisable to return to consult and
> in order to have an understanding with Flint?)

There is a French counterpart to the Smithsonian Air and Space Museum; it occupies the former passenger terminal buildings at the old Le Bourget airport, a thirty-minute train ride from the center of Paris.

Outside the Musée de l'Air et de l'Espace, the large Breitling clock—a showy version of the aviator's wristwatch—is an hour slow. Three Mirage jet fighters, poised on poles, appear ready to flare into the rainy sky. Ariane space rockets, now decommissioned, rise behind the museum. They grace the airfield where Charles Lindbergh landed in 1927 after his transatlantic solo flight.

The first fragile and graceful French aircraft are here. Replicas of the early gliders, and tiny bird- and batlike planes. The *oiseaux artificiels*—artificial birds—are gathered in memory of legendary French builders and flyers: Farnam, Blériot, Voisin, Garros, and Monsieur Santos-Dumont (French by affection). By 1910 or so, the airplanes seem sleeker, more competent, moving from biplane to single wing, from open frames to fuselage.

Schoolchildren, visiting in groups, laugh at a vintage film showing a man with a parachute jumping from the first stage of the Eiffel Tower. He dies, we learn, as we watch him fall too fast. The final frame is of a gouge in the ground.

The film reel featuring the pilot Adolphe Pégoud draws quieter attention. Pégoud is flying a Blériot at a 1913 airshow. He flies—and this has not been done before—a controlled inside-out loop. The plane is upside down at the top. Pégoud lands, and hundreds of well-dressed men and women race across the field to greet him. The film explains that Pégoud got the idea when he was testing a parachute design. He took off, reached altitude, and jumped. The plane was being sacrificed for the test, and as Pégoud was drifting down he watched his craft spinning along by itself, even flying upside down. He asked Louis Blériot to build him a reinforced plane so he could do it himself.

Pégoud said, "I wanted to demonstrate to pilots that no matter what happens the aeroplane does not necessarily have to drop; given mastery of oneself, a simple maneuver will make the aeroplane reassume its normal position."

The museum has a modest Wright brothers exhibit featuring a 1903 Flyer replica and sketching the story of later accomplishments, but in this building the glory is to France.

I meet up with Stéphane Nicolaou, a staff historian at the museum. He wonders, looking back, what would have happened if the Wrights had flown in France earlier than 1908.

"They were geniuses, that's no doubt. But from this foundation you have to grow up and up and up and they were not ready for that. If they'd come in 1905 it would have been a tremendous success because development of aviation in Europe was too slow. France had fantastic designers, but the engine was not there. If you have not the engine, you have only a glider."

He pulls out files of photographs. "Have you seen these of Wilbur in Le Mans?" There are hundreds, and even more from Pau, the resort town in southern France where Wilbur flew early in 1909. Pictures of Wilbur at his plane and in the air, Wilbur with royalty, Wilbur with kids—and his adopted dog, Flyer, who shared his living space inside the wooden hangar.

Stéphane says, "I'll show you a favorite." He finds a book. "This is Lartigue. Do you know Lartigue's work? He was a child prodigy, taking photos."

Jacques Henri Lartigue's family was rich, with homes in both Paris and the country. From age six, he had a camera—film and developing chemicals came from the neighborhood pharmacy—

and his photographs sparkle with his excitement. His "first photo taken absolutely by myself with my 13 × 18 cm plate camera" was in 1902.

Lartigue chased across the landscape after balloons and biplanes, and in 1909, at age fifteen, he traveled to Pau in hopes of seeing the American flyer:

> Wilbur is my favorite hero. The newspapers are telling me about the Wright brothers. That they fly for several minutes, maybe even twenty minutes! That they turn in the air, that they ramble [*se promener*]! And land! Often without breaking their airplane!!!?? Wilbur Wright has almost replaced Buffalo Bill and Nick Carter in my heart.
>
> My little Gaumont notepad hidden in my hand, I approach a bit. Wilbur has gone into his hangar; he comes back out.
>
> He has put on his cap, "Wilbur-style." Two fellows, maybe mechanics, have seen me. They prowl around me. I continue. Wilbur looks at me and, all of a sudden, turns his back on me! He speaks his American gibberish. He may be furious, but the photo is taken; that consoles me a bit for the bad weather that prevents us from seeing him fly.

Now, almost a century later, you can look at a thousand pictures and not see one that resembles Lartigue's. The caption is "Wilbur Wright *et sa fameuse casquette*."

The photograph is lustrous black and white, showing Wilbur in a side view from the waist up, wearing a heavy coat, a collar and tie, and indeed, the cloth workingman's cap that the French had come to adore. A wing of his plane is in softer focus in the background.

Wilbur stands with his right fist propped on his hip. His head is inclined slightly down; his right eye appears barely open. Deep lines of fatigue mark his cheek. He has been flying practically every day since August. The photographer believed Wilbur was angry, but as you look at the picture, you think, What could a fifteen-year old know of this moment?

After an hour's fast train ride west from Paris, I am in a bar in Le Mans, the old cathedral city surrounded by farmland—that is now famous for "the Twenty-four Hours of Le Mans," the motor-racing spectacle that began in 1923. Of Wilbur Wright the town makes scant mention, except for a Rue Wilbur Wright, and a somewhat grandiose ode-to-flight statue near the town center. I wanted to find, and did after much asking, the first Wright memorial. It's a rectangular piece of granite, standing nine feet high. The edges are roughly carved. At the center there's an image of an eagle's upswept wings, and the inscription À WILBUR WRIGHT.

This monument once stood at a fork in the road out in the country and took some hits during World War II—you can see where the large-caliber shells shattered chunks out of the stone. In 1980 the marker was brought into Le Mans and set up on the street outside the former site of Léon Bollée's automobile factory.

At the bar another beer arrives, and a small man with a gray ponytail climbs up on the stool next to me. He lights a cigarette and smiles, lifts his glass. We manage some conversation. Somehow the name Elvis comes up. My friend grabs my arm and holds a hand over his heart and sings, "Tomorrow, tomorrow"—which is from the musical *Annie,* but he's so close to tears that I don't mention it. He tells me that Le Mans is a truly wonderful place, and, looking straight in my eyes, says, "I am the pretty little voice of Le Mans."

I tell him why I've come to his city.

"Oh . . . Veelbur Wright."

His smile is close to rapture, and he takes my notebook and asks for a pen to write this in English about Wilbur:

"You are our Master! Beautiful!"

The next morning, Friday, is the city's market day. The parking lot of Cathédrale St-Julien fills with vendors—white asparagus, radishes, rabbits, a hundred cheeses. Plus antique postcards:

I ask one dealer, "Wilbur Wright?"

"*Oui,*" he says, starting to pull boxes out of his van. I shuffle through the cards, all of which are in plastic slips. He has three hundred or so cards here, and only a few are duplicates. I buy six, including a hand-tinted pastel view of Wilbur's plane in the air, with cars and bicycles below. Most of the postcards are blank on the back, having never been mailed.

Wilbur had first traveled to Le Mans in early June of 1908, when he returned to France after agreeing to an offer from a Paris-based syndicate. Wright Flyers would be made and sold in France; Orville and Wilbur would get cash up front, would own much of the company, and would earn royalties. But there were two stipulations: they had to make successful demonstration flights and agree to train French pilots.

Wilbur and his French agent took the train out to Le Mans to meet Léon Bollée, the automaker and aviation enthusiast who had written to Wilbur, saying, come fly your airplane here, we'll take care of you. In a letter to Katharine, Wilbur commented on Bollée's generosity, explaining that he had "placed at our disposition a large room in which we can proceed at once to assemble the machine."

Wilbur explored the countryside around Le Mans and decided the flying could be done at a horse racing track a few miles from town, telling Orville, "We get exclusive possession of the race course at 250 francs per month and 15% of gate receipts if we charge admission at any time. The course is 800 meters long and 300 meters wide. The ground is not at all smooth but will do for landing all right. There are several trees at one corner which will prevent following the track all the way around unless I go over them."

The airplane arrived in June 1908, in crates from the port at Le Havre. It had been shipped over the previous fall. Orville had done the packing in Dayton, carefully. But French customs officials had industriously inspected the contents and made a grand mess. Not realizing that, Wilbur blamed his brother in a letter dated June 17:

"I opened the boxes yesterday and have been puzzled ever since to know how you could have wasted two whole days packing them. I am sure that with a scoop shovel I could have put things in within two or three minutes and made fully as good a job of it. . . . Ten or a dozen ribs were broken, the radiators are badly smashed . . . and I suspect the axle is bent a little. It is going to take much longer to get ready than it should have done if things had been in better shape."

The summer weeks went by as Wilbur tried to sew and fit and

bang the machine together, working mostly alone. In an accident while testing the engine, he scalded his left arm and the side of his chest. In letters home, Wilbur joked about the amateurish medical treatment; all along he'd been trying to reassure his sister that things were fine and quite interesting in Le Mans:

"No one in the hotel understands my English or my French, but they do their best to serve me well. . . . I was a little astonished and disturbed the other evening when I sat down to dinner to find my soup, which was a sort of noodle soup, turning into all sorts of curious forms and even letters of the alphabet. I began to think I had the 'jim jams.' On close investigation I found that the dough had been run through forms so as to make the different letters of the alphabet and the figures too! It was like looking into the 'hell box' of a printing office, and was all the more amusing because every mouthful of soup taken out, brought up a new combination."

The summer of 1908 was the first time one of the Wright brothers had flown without the other nearby. While Wilbur continued his work in France, Orville remained in Dayton, getting ready to take a second airplane to Fort Myer, across the Potomac River from Washington, D.C. The U.S. War Department had accepted a bid by the Wrights to supply a plane, and this contract also required demonstration flights. The brothers were apprehensive—they would be on separate flying fields, working an ocean's distance apart.

Orville wrote to Wilbur in Le Mans, "I am expecting every day to hear that you have begun experiments. Be very careful in your first flights. I think there will be little danger after you get accustomed to the new levers."

Later, Wilbur cautioned Orville, "In your flights at Washington I think you should be careful to begin practice in calms and *keep well above the ground*. You will probably be unable to cut as short curves as I do here, but you will have it easier on your speed test in a straight line."

I find a taxi and ask to go to Les Hunaudières—the racetrack. The driver looks back in his mirror. "Twenty-four hours?"

"No, not the cars, the old horse racing track."

"Ah, yes," he says, and we start off.

He just as well could have said, it's no longer there. I've been worried that Les Hunaudières could now be the name of a countryside housing development, or that the land might have been paved over for factory space.

We drive south from Le Mans, and about four miles out we turn off the highway onto a sandy gravel road. My heart lifts— I can see a small grandstand ahead, and a dirt track and a grass infield. We stop beside a small varnished-wood ticket booth that easily could have been here in 1908. I walk out onto the wide racetrack and find hoofprints in the almost-pink dusty earth— they run in a clockwise direction around the oval, which is banked at the turns. Trees circle the track, poplars and chestnuts, and beyond, apple orchards and cattle, a farmhouse. It's quiet, as it must have been in 1908. Les Hunaudières suited Wilbur's needs just fine. He wrote to his father, "I am now staying at the shed at the race course . . . while the weather lasts I will be reasonably comfortable. We get dinner and supper at a little cafe nearby and make 'caffe au lait' ourselves in the morning."

As I stand on the dirt track I am taken back to a moment I have glimpsed in the faded blacks and yellowing whites of photographs. The grandstand, the grass, and Wilbur's plane set for takeoff. Ladies with showy hats, men with boaters. It is the late afternoon of August 8. It's a Saturday and there's been word that Wilbur might fly. Perhaps a hundred people have come. Several of the French aviators are here. The airplane is taken from the shed—coming out sideways, slowly and carefully—and moved by cart to midfield. Wilbur, in business dress as usual, is silent. He walks around the craft, touching, tightening. He and a helper spin the propellers to start the engine. He takes his seat. And flies.

Wilbur made two circuits of the field, but the crowd was startled right at the beginning when he had to make a deep, banking turn to miss the trees—the French had never seen an airplane do that.

In the days ahead, thousands would travel to Le Mans and Les Hunaudières. Sunday's *Le Figaro* newspaper called Wilbur's first flight in France "a revolution in the scientific world." And the flyer Léon Delagrange said, *"Nous sommes battus"*—We are beaten.

Wilbur did not celebrate that night; it was reported he was seen sleeping in the shed, next to his plane. He wrote his own account in a letter home the next day, saying, "I finished the machine yesterday far enough to enable me to make a little flight. Neither my arm nor the machine was really finished but a report got out that I would make the first trial yesterday and a number of people had come down from Paris, including two Russian officers who have been waiting there for several weeks by instruction of their government. As the day for a first trial was the finest we have had for several weeks, I thought it would be a good thing to do a little something."

Wilbur flew almost daily; often he'd be up for twenty minutes. He began to be frustrated by reporters and photographers as well as by the crowds of people who showed up expecting him to fly. It was hard to find time to rest, or repair his plane. Orville, test-flying at Fort Myer with the help of two mechanics, got off to an impressive start, setting new world records for both altitude and duration, often circling for more than an hour. Wilbur was following the news about his brother in the French newspapers.

Then, on September 17, Orville's plane crashed to the ground at Fort Myer. He was severely injured, and a passenger he had taken up, Army Lieutenant Thomas Selfridge, was killed. A message was delivered to Wilbur at the racetrack, and those who saw the envelope—*le papier bleu*—knew it was bad news. Wilbur rode his bike into town to wait for the next cablegram—it said his brother would live.

That fall, as Orville recuperated at Fort Myer, Wilbur continued his trials at Le Mans, making more than a hundred flights, often with passengers. A British newspaper had offered a prize for the first flight across the English Channel, but the brothers, although intrigued by the notion of a channel flight, decided not to take the risk. It was the Michelin Cup Wilbur wanted, even though he'd miss going home for Christmas. The *Coupe Michelin* would be awarded, along with 20,000 francs, to the pilot who made the longest flight of 1908. Back on September 21, Wilbur had stayed up for an hour and a half. It didn't seem likely that anyone else could beat that, but he wanted to be sure, and on the thirty-first of December, in an icy rain, Wilbur flew his plane around a circuit for ninety miles and more than two hours and twenty minutes.

CHAPTER SIX

FORT MYER

I HAVE A TRUSTED COMPANION AS I WANDER ABOUT THE LAST century. Bishop Milton Wright's brief, quotidian notations are reassuring; he's trying to keep his family safe and close. I take my copy of his *Diaries* from the shelf to see what the bishop had been thinking as his sons began the demonstration flights in France and at Fort Myer:

August 19, 1908: "Orville started to Washington City, this evening at 10:12, via Harrisburg, Pa. Both he and Wilbur peril their lives, perhaps Orville most by the unsuitableness of the grounds at Ft. Myer."

It is time to go see where Orville flew. I drive across the Potomac River, past the Pentagon, and along the ridge at the crest of Arlington National Cemetery. Fort Myer, at the cemetery's western edge, has a Civil War heritage, standing on high ground with artillery-range views of the capital and its approaches. Today you look down over the hillsides of white grave markers to the Lincoln Memorial across the Potomac, and beyond to the Washington Monument and the White House.

I turn in at the main gate, clear security, and meet army historian Kim Holien at the reviewing stand on the edge of the parade ground. Holien is a civilian, the first historian ever at Fort Myer. As we talk, I notice he has a special awareness of sounds around us. The rifle shots I've been hearing? "A twenty-one-gun salute. Seven rifles—M-14s—firing three volleys. Those are members of The Old Guard, practicing for funerals." And I'd just seen the smoke and heard several blasts from long, narrow black guns recoiling on their carriages. Holien says, "The howitzers are used for ceremonies—they're modified to take 75-millimeter blank shells." In years past, the Fort Myer guns would be fired when important visitors arrived to see the president. On the White House lawn they'd hear the distant *cruumph,* floating across the river valley.

"That's a Huey," Holien says, referring to the steely throb of a helicopter passing overhead. "It's got that little missing beat in the synchronization. We hear that all the time, along with the planes out of Reagan National, and I always think back to when you didn't hear *anything* in the air. I did an oral history interview with Polly Miller, who was the last person left alive who had seen Orville Wright fly here, and one of the things she remembered most was the sound. She described it as this slow *womph, womph, womph* sound. It was those huge wooden propellers. Who'd ever heard a sound like that? It was like hearing the first jet go overhead."

For the United States Army in 1908, if it was in the air, it belonged to the Signal Corps, which started using balloons in the Civil War. But there was now an aeronautical division, negotiating with Orville and Wilbur for an airplane. Twenty-five thousand dollars was the agreed-upon price, far less than what the Wrights wanted, and even that required Wilbur's attention in Washington. An open bidding process was mandated by the government, and it appears that the Wrights helped write the specifications.

To satisfy the army, the flying machine must carry "two persons having a combined weight of 350 pounds." A speed trial would be held, with a flying start and a flying finish. Forty miles an hour was the target, with a deduction for less and a bonus for more. There was also an endurance test, during which the plane must be "under perfect control and equilibrium."

Looking ahead, the army wanted a plane that could be taken apart and carried on a wagon, with an assembly time of one hour. It should be designed to "ascend in any country which may be encountered in field service . . . and land in a field without requiring a specially prepared spot." However, there was a requirement that would, as it turned out, be overlooked at Fort Myer: "It should be provided with some device to permit of a safe descent in case of an accident to the propelling machinery."

The single sheet of paper that's been called the birth certificate of the United States Air Force was issued on February 10, 1908. The original is in a glass display case at Wright State University:

> Requisition Order 3619
> Wright Brothers, Dayton, Ohio
> Item: One (1) heavier-than-air flying machine, at $25,000.00. Goods must be securely packed for shipment and delivered within 200 days . . . to Fort Myer, Va.

✤ ✤

The present-day Fort Myer parade ground is about the size of a soccer field. In 1908 the open land was twenty-five times larger, a long rectangle, mostly used for cavalry training. At the time there were 1,500 horses on the post. Still, Orville's flying space would be more confined than it was at Huffman Prairie, as well as on the field outside Le Mans, where Wilbur was flying.

"Right at that flagpole is approximately the spot where Orville would take off," Holien says. "He was starting south and there's an escarpment there, about a ten-foot drop, so he was shooting off that little piece of high ground."

The officers and their families living in the handsome red brick homes that stand in a row facing away from the parade grounds could have seen the takeoffs and landings from a kitchen window. The three-story Victorian duplexes are still there, now prestige addresses for generals.

Holien points to the building just beyond the flagpole. "That building over there with the white front porches and railings is our post headquarters. That was the hospital, where Lieutenant Selfridge died and where Wright stayed until he went back home."

Orville had arrived in Washington on August 20. The airplane, which had been shipped to the Arlington train station, had come in that morning. The army provided workspace in a balloon hangar. Both Charlie Taylor and Charles Furnas, another mechanic friend of the Wrights, came from Dayton to help.

From the Signal Corps' "Log of Wright's Aeroplane":

August 26: "Small details and connections being made."

August 27: "Engine run. Chains, cases, and thrust rods not properly aligned. Bronze bearings for thrust rods on end main shaft bent. Engine stopped after 10 sec. Happened twice."

August 28: "Hot bearings. No grease cups on end axle bearings."

August 29: "Engine skipping [on] acct [of] poor gasoline. Bearing still gets too *hot*. Magneto giving trouble."

August 31: "Engine being run to ease."

On that day Orville wrote to Katharine, "I don't know whether you have seen the Washington papers or not. The reporters seem to think I am not in the least uneasy about fulfilling our contract. They say that I do no boasting of what I can do; that they can get but little out of me as to what I expect to accomplish, but that I have the air of perfect confidence!

"I am meeting some very handsome young ladies! I will have an awful time trying to think of their names if I meet them again. . . . I think it quite probable that I will make an attempt to fly tomorrow evening."

Orville had taken a room at the Cosmos Club, then located on Lafayette Square at the center of downtown Washington, a meeting place for politicians, scientists, scholars, and explorers. Staying here, Orville could have been tempted to envision himself within the scope of history: the White House is a scant block away. Daniel Webster, Henry Clay, James and Dolley Madison— all names from his childhood—had lived on the square.

On the morning of September 3, Orville might have awakened early, hearing the clip-clop of horses in the street below, or a passing automobile. If he was worried, there was reason. Except for the not-so-reassuring efforts that spring in North Carolina— the brothers practiced some in Kitty Hawk—he hadn't flown in two and a half years, and Wilbur was now far off in France.

We can assume Orville dressed in a well-cut suit, polished his shoes, went downstairs for breakfast, perhaps looked at the newspapers. What is known is that he boarded an electric street-car, rode to Fort Myer, and took to the air in the late afternoon. From the flight log: "Distance covered: went around drill grounds once and a half. Maximum height: 35 feet. Speed: 36 miles an hour. Time in flight: 1'11"."

Kim Holien takes me into his office to show me a videotape copy of a treasure. Two years ago he heard the words that are every historian's dream: "Hey, I found something down here in the throw-out bin and it says 'Wright Brothers' on it." It was an old-style three-quarter-inch videotape, with clear, well-photographed images of a Wright airplane in flight over Fort Myer. Kim took the tape to the Smithsonian's National Air and Space Museum. He remembers, "The first guy there started the movie up and said, 'Ho-hum, this is the Alexander Graham Bell footage, we know this.' Then he sees something brand-new and gets on the phone and says, 'Boss, you'd better get down here.' And that guy comes and then he calls, 'Big boss, you'd better get down here.'"

The inventor of the telephone, in the seeming interest of collegial research, showed up at Fort Myer with two cameramen. Dr. Bell had been earnestly and expensively involved in aeronautics, starting with kites made from assemblages of triangular cells that resembled a honeycomb. The structures—some of them huge—were impractical, and Bell's team moved on to powered glider craft with some success. Bell's moviemaking at Fort Myer would document a dramatic moment in the arc of aviation and also provide his own engineers with close-up information about the Wrights' machine.

The version of Bell's Fort Myer footage that has been widely seen came from what the archivists call "Camera A." The version that Kim Holien's staff turned up includes material from "Camera B." The original "B" film actually resides, deep and mostly forgotten, within the National Archives. Someone, somewhere, had edited "A" and "B" footage together to make a six-and-a half-minute movie of Orville Wright's flight testing at Fort Myer. Robert Clark, a film archivist at the Air and Space Museum, recalls the moment Kim Holien's movie came up on the screen: "Its clarity and completeness was astonishing. It had scenes I had never seen before." The new footage helps extend the visual narrative, adding tension, as Orville appears to fly the oval course in almost real time.

The film, shot in the summer of 1909, opens with several men in suits and straw boater hats gathering outside the door of a shed. One man has the privileged manner of a reporter, with a folded newspaper in his coat pocket. Several soldiers can be seen, and a French military officer wearing a white kepi, the round cap with turned-down brim. There's only one woman in the scenes, mysteriously attractive and wearing a long, light-colored dress and a hat. President William Howard Taft lumbers into camera range, hands behind his back, straw hat tilted on his head. At 330 pounds, and as the previous Secretary of War, Taft would have a certain presence on this field, but he seems just like one of the guys.

The Flyer is lifted sideways from the shed and swung around to face the field. A large wheel is placed under it, and seven soldiers push the machine along to the takeoff point. It would have been difficult for spectators to know which way this airplane was supposed to go. Two propellers in the rear. Two fabric-covered panels set horizontally in the front; they look as if they could be the tail. A second look teaches you—the large twin wooden landing skids rise in a grand curve to protect the *front* of the plane.

An army officer is shown settling onto the seat on the bottom wing. Orville appears, checking connections and the tension of wires. He unsnaps the brim of his cap, snugs it down, and, facing the plane, puts his left knee on a brace to swing neatly around and sit beside his passenger.

The props are pulled down and through their arc to start the engine. They come to speed, turning in opposite directions to balance the torque. Takeoff is boosted by the weight-drop system devised at Huffman Prairie, and used by Wilbur in France. The ground crew soldiers are now strung out along a rope, hauling the weights up inside the derrick with four poles meeting at the top. The weights fall, the rope flings the Flyer forward along its wooden track, and Orville rides out the first shallow dips before gaining some altitude. First a bank to the left that swings into a full rising turn. Orville keeps the stone wall of Arlington Cemetery fifty feet below his right wingtip. Then two turns at the narrow end of the drill field and a run along the stables and the barracks. The propellers appear to spin slowly, flashing white against the dark of the trees. Altitude is reached in slow measure—the 1909 Wright Flyer is not a plane that will leap into the air and zoom off cross-country.

With Orville at one hundred feet, the camera shows the cemetery wall, as well as the spectators, carriages, and autos. Also a flickering glimpse of several interurban streetcars stopped to watch the flight. The crowds increased at Fort Myer as Orville began setting records. A world endurance mark: fifty-seven and a half minutes. Altitude, two hundred feet. Then he flew six minutes with a passenger, his friend and official observer Lieutenant Frank Lahm, establishing a two-person record. And an even longer solo: seventy-four minutes. Then higher still: 310 feet. Five thousand people watched from below. Polly Miller, Kim Holien's eyewitness, was perched on the red stone cemetery wall on perhaps one of those days. She was nine years old. Polly remembered the sound of the props, the bang of the weights dropping, and said of the plane, "It looked like a big cage in the air. There wasn't anything solid about it, you know, excepting where they sat. The rest of it was just wires and canvas. It seemed so small to me. It looked to me like it was awfully dangerous." And surely it was.

Army First Lieutenant Thomas Selfridge was a West Point graduate from San Francisco, and was sent to Fort Myer to be one of the observers for the Signal Corps. He was also an aeronautical competitor of the Wrights, and for that reason Orville didn't want to take him flying. On September 6 he wrote to Wilbur, saying the lieutenant was to leave Fort Myer soon for a dirigible exhibition: "I will be glad to have Selfridge out of the way. I don't trust him an inch. He is intensely interested in the subject, and plans to meet me often at dinners, etc., where he can try to pump me. He has a good education, and a clear mind. I understand that he does a good deal of knocking behind my back."

Selfridge was intrigued by Alexander Graham Bell's experiments with lifting kites, and traveled to the Bell summer compound in Nova Scotia to learn more. Glenn Hammond Curtiss was there, a champion motorcycle racer and engine builder. Bell soon formed the Aerial Experiment Association with Curtiss, Selfridge, and two other young men. Near the end of 1907, Tom Selfridge became a pilot, rising 168 feet above a lake at the controls of a kite with a forty-two-foot wingspan; the *Cygnet* was towed into the air by a boat and, with the help of a strong wind, stayed aloft for seven minutes.

Selfridge designed the next AEA craft, a conventionally powered biplane. Curtiss built the motor and flew the *Red Wing* 318 feet. The group's third powered machine, the *June Bug,* won a prize for straight-line flight, traveling more than five thousand feet in one minute and forty seconds. The AEA's planes used ailerons—small wing sections that can be moved up and down—for turning and banking control and overall balance. The Wright brothers believed their 1904 wing-warping patent was being violated by the AEA's design, maintaining that any technique for controlling an aircraft by changing the shape of the wing surface would be an infringement.

From Bishop Milton Wright's diary, September 17, 1908: "Orville injured. Orville's disaster at 5:00; Selfridge's death."

I walk the fort's parade grounds, trying to imagine the flight that late Thursday afternoon, a cool day with light winds. The start would have been there by the flagpole. Lieutenant Selfridge, it's reported, took off his uniform jacket and campaign hat and sat down on the thin, narrow seat next to Orville.

With the engine exhaust explosions bouncing back from the brick buildings on either side of the field, the plane left the end of the rail, dipping once almost to the grass. Tom Selfridge, at 175 pounds, was the heaviest passenger Orville had tried to carry.

I continue south to stand in a parking lot not far from the boundary of Arlington Cemetery. Kim Holien had shown me the spot where it's believed the plane hit the ground. Orville made three turns around his oval course, climbed to 100 feet, steered for a wider turn. Those below heard two thumping noises, saw the plane shake, and noticed that Orville had cut off the motor. A propeller blade had split apart, losing power and setting up a vibration that led to the jamming of the rudder. The spectators watched as the left wing fell and the right wing rose.

Orville described it later: "Quick as a flash, the machine turned down in front and started straight for the ground. Our course for fifty feet was within a very few degrees of perpendicular. Lieutenant Selfridge up to this time had not uttered a word, though he took a hasty glance behind when the propeller broke, and turned once or twice to look into my face, evidently to see what I thought of the situation. But when the machine turned headfirst for the ground, he exclaimed 'Oh! Oh!' in an almost inaudible voice. Suddenly just before reaching the ground . . . the machine began to right itself rapidly. A few feet more, and we would have landed safely."

Three army surgeons were watching, and ran to the crash. A mounted cavalry officer tried to hold back the crowd. Selfridge and Orville were pulled from the dusty tangle of splintered wood and ripped fabric and taken by stretcher to the post hospital. Lieutenant Selfridge, never regaining consciousness, died that night of a fractured skull, a victim of the first fatal accident in a powered aircraft.

Orville's brother Wilbur, a few days after receiving the cablegram about the crash, and having read the newspaper accounts that reached Le Mans, wrote to his father:

"I received the news of Orville's accident. . . . I know that you will be more cut up over the affair than even we are. Young peo-

ple are shocked for a moment but soon recover themselves. You
need not fear that such a thing will happen again. It is the only
time that anything has broken on any of our machines while in
flight, in 9 year's experience. . . . I think the trouble was caused
by the feverish conditions under which Orville had to work. His
time was consumed by people who wished to congratulate and
encourage him when the thing he really needed was time to rest
and time to work. He is too courteous to refuse to see people. . . . I will never leave him alone in such a position again."

Katharine left Dayton in time to arrive the next day. A Signal
Corps automobile brought her from Washington's Union
Station to Fort Myer. Orville, she learned, had a broken left
thigh, cracked ribs, and a back injury. Katharine wrote to her
brother Lorin on September 19:

> I found Orville looking pretty badly. His face is cut in
> several places, the deepest gash being over his left eye. His
> leg had just been set, yesterday afternoon. He was looking
> for me, and when I went in his chin quivered and the tears
> came to his eyes but he soon braced up again. The shock
> has weakened him very much, of course. The only time
> that he showed any sign of breaking down was when he
> asked me if I knew that Lieut. Selfridge was dead.
>
> They gave him drugs, to give him some rest Thursday
> night. . . . Yesterday morning he was comfortable but in
> the afternoon when I saw him, he was very nervous. I
> supposed the working with his leg had made him so. I
> bathed that part of his face that was exposed, and his
> chest and shoulders. That quieted him, some.

He has a nice nurse, and both doctor and nurse are devoted to him. I found the room well filled with flowers and a great basket of lovely fruit. Last night, there came a telegram to Orville, from the High School, saying: "The thousand proud pupils and teachers of Steele High School unanimously extend sympathy and encouragement."

Katharine was on leave from her teaching job, and took care of Orville throughout his seven weeks in the Fort Myer hospital. She roomed with friends across the river in Washington, an hour's trolley ride away, but spent all her days and many nights in a chair by Orville's bed.

On September 21 she wrote to her father about the news of Wilbur's flying in France:

Will had his nerve with him today sure enough. One hour, thirty-one minutes, twenty-five seconds! All the newspaper men began calling up the Hospital to tell me. Orville did a great deal of smiling over it. That did him an immense amount of good.

It is midnight now and I am very tired. Orville is still sleeping. The night nurse has gone down to get a sandwich and some tea for me. Tonight is going much better than last night. Your letter and money came all right today. . . . I telegraphed Mrs. Wagner to have my gingham dress finished and sent on. I don't want to be shabby for brother's sake. . . . Sorry to leave you alone so long."

On September 24, from a table in Orville's hospital room, Katharine wrote to reassure Wilbur in Le Mans:

I shall not leave him until he is out of this place or at least until he does not need such careful attention. School can go and my salary, too. I have already lost a week. But little bubbo shall not be neglected as long as I am able to crawl around. . . . Lieutenant Selfridge is to be buried tomorrow at Arlington. His family has come in from California. I sent my cards as soon as they arrived and we have sent flowers for the funeral.

The wrecked Flyer had been put under guard in its shed, waiting for shipment to Dayton; the engine and many of the control parts could—and would—be used again. The army assured Katharine and Orville that the demonstration flights could continue the next summer. And Major George Squier told reporters, "If Mr. Wright should never again enter an airplane, his work last week at Fort Myer will have secured him a lasting place in history as the man who showed the world that mechanical flight was an assured success. . . . The problem is solved, and it only remains to work out the details."

Orville Wright's accomplishments at Fort Myer are handsomely noted with a monument at the parade ground's reviewing stand, and the Wright Gate serves as a post entrance. But the Selfridge Gate is the one that you might hear mentioned with a note of reverence. It's a few steps away from the crash site, an arched, gated opening into Arlington National Cemetery. I notice that it's kept locked. A bronze plaque notes that Lieutenant Selfridge was the "first military officer in the world to pilot an airplane, solo. . . . Had he lived he would have been one of our Army's most brilliant leaders in aeronautics."

Thomas Selfridge was buried with full military honors in the cemetery just beyond the gate.

From Bishop Wright's diary, Sunday, November 1: "Orville and Katharine came home from Fort Myer, Va., arriving at 9:00 a.m. He is brought out from the depot on a wheeled chair. His mind is good as ever and his body promises to be in due time." Later in the month, Orville got an invitation from his brother in France: "I very strongly suggest that you and Kate, and Pop too if he will, should come over to Europe immediately. It is important to get machines ready for the spring business and the spring and winter races. You could superintend and design, when you could not actually work. There is more to be done than I can do, even if I stay. Can't you come over for a couple of months? I do not see how I can get home, and yet I am crazy to see some of the home folks and to have some consultation with you."

The reunion was January 12, 1909, early in the morning in Paris. Back then, train stations were the setting for just this sort of scene. A swirl of steam, and then there's Wilbur, tanned and strong after six months of flying—he'd gained weight, and it pleased him. Katharine appears dressed for travel, looking around expectantly. Orville, pale and smiling, refuses help and uses two canes to steady his steps to the platform. The three siblings link arms and walk out into the city. It is Katharine's first trip to Europe.

Wilbur moved his operations to Pau, a once-fashionable resort city in southern France. The climate was kinder there, and he'd been offered a house and workshop, the services of a chef, and a large open flying field. Orville and Katharine were given a suite at a luxury hotel at no cost, because the hotel wanted to capitalize on the Wrights' presence and thus attract new vacation business to Pau.

Pilot training was Wilbur's main concern, and he worked intensively with three students, two of whom made long solo flights in March. However, Wilbur and his plane were famous in France, and now his co-inventor brother and their sister could be seen as well. The Wrights were sudden, starry celebrities. And the elite of Europe traveled to Pau to see them. Edward VII arrived from England, and King Alfonso of Spain. Lords and ladies came, military leaders, captains of industry and barons of banking. To say that you were in Pau in the late winter of 1909 was to suggest that you flew with Wilbur, helped launch his plane, joked with Orville, or perhaps kissed Katharine's hand.

After France came Italy, and a series of demonstration flights at Centocelle. Then back to France and England, for parties and banquets and gold medals. A magazine reported on one gathering in Paris:

> The occasion was made an opportunity for handing over the Michelin Prize of 20,000 francs, the auspicious moment being reserved for the arrival of dessert. M. Michelin rose, and in a suitable speech made the presentation, which came as an agreeable surprise to those present.
>
> Wilbur Wright, having expressed his thanks, calmly divided the banknotes into two packets, and without a word handed over one of them to his brother, while he put the other in his own pocket. This little act, done without ostentation and in the most natural manner possible,

served to emphasize beyond anything that has yet taken place, the real partnership which exists between these two Americans as a result of their long years of pioneer labor.

The bishop's diary, May 5, 1909: "The children sailed for New York on the *Kron Prinzesion Cecile,* due at New York next Tuesday."

Milton Wright had just seen his son Wilbur—who'd been away from home for an entire year—in a newsreel at a downtown movie theater, and he noted his own encounter with fame: "Called for my envelopes at the Post Office. They recognize and honor me as father of the Wright brothers with considerable ado. 'Do they discard all use of tobacco,' [they] asked. 'Yes, and all whiskey!' I replied."

There was a big welcome at the dock in Hoboken, and another one at the train station in Dayton. In Washington two weeks later, all three Wrights were honored with a luncheon at the Cosmos Club, followed by a White House meeting with President Taft.

The brothers were worried about the Fort Myer trials, which were soon set to resume, and tried to finish a new and stronger Flyer. However, Dayton wasn't finished celebrating and would not be denied. The official homecoming was set: June 17 and 18. Parades and a pageant and fireworks and a ceremony at the fairgrounds with two thousand five hundred red-white-and-blue-dressed school children forming an American flag. Fifteen members of the Wright family were there. Bishop Wright gave the invocation. Orville and Wilbur, wearing top hats and morning coats, accepted their well-meant gold and diamond medals. Two weeks later Wilbur complained in a letter to Octave Chanute: "The Dayton presentation has been made the excuse for an elaborate carnival and advertisement of the city under the guise of being an honor to us. As it was done in spite of our known wishes, we are not as appreciative as we might have been."

By late June the Wrights had their sturdier and faster 1909 Army Flyer on the field at Fort Myer. The first tests were discouraging. The machine didn't want to lift, and then didn't want to stay up. One of the skids cracked during a landing. On July 2, Orville hit a tree with his right wing while trying to land after the engine had stopped. The fall was hard, the damage extensive, and Orville was unnerved but unhurt. Wilbur became furious at a photographer who had rushed to the scene, and threw a broken piece of the airplane's frame at him. He later apologized when he learned the man was taking pictures for the War Department.

Soon, though, Orville, with Wilbur leading the ground crew, was again setting records at Fort Myer. The big test was the speed trial. It was to be cross-country, a ten-mile round trip with an observer on board. The previous summer Orville had done some scouting: "I went over the grounds for five miles in several directions from the Fort. I have decided on a course directly toward Alexandria."

The Potomac River would be in sight, going and coming. The starting altitude would be 240 feet above sea level, with the turning point at 160 feet. Orville noted, "There would be quite a number of good landing places . . . though there is one large forest of over a mile wide in which there are no breaks whatsoever."

Army Lieutenant Benjamin Foulois was picked to fly with Orville; he was told the day before. Lieutenant Foulois mapped out the course to Alexandria with a turnaround over a high point known as Shooter's Hill. He had a telephone and a telegraph line installed so a signal could be sent when the plane reached Alexandria, and asked the Signal Corps to raise captive balloons at Shooter's Hill and at the midway point with Fort Myer.

In his autobiography, Foulois wrote, "I would like to think that I was chosen on the basis of intellectual and technical ability, but I found out later that it was my short stature, light weight, and map-reading experience that tipped the decision in my favor."

Foulois, at 126 pounds, climbed on board with two stopwatches, a barometer, a compass, and a map. They took off, circled to 125 feet, and came back over the center of the field, where Wilbur waved a flag and the time officially started. The young lieutenant pointed the way. He wrote:

> We reached Shooter's Hill all right, and I flicked the second stopwatch. There was a crowd on the brow of the hill, and I could see them wave their umbrellas and handkerchiefs. It seemed to me that the angle of bank of the plane was awfully steep as we rounded the turn and the wing tip was much too close to the tops of the trees. A downdraft hit us, and I thought we were going to cartwheel into them for sure. We straightened out, however, and started back for Myer. Going down wind now, our ground speed increased and Orville climbed until we reached 400 feet—a world's altitude record. As we neared Myer, Orville nosed down to pick up speed and aimed at the starting tower. I flicked the stopwatch off as we crossed the starting line and relaxed as he made a circle over Arlington Cemetery, cut off the engine, and glided in for a fairly smooth landing amid a cloud of dust. Wilbur rushed up to us, and it was the first time I ever saw him with a smile on his face."

All the stopwatch times were averaged. Orville had flown the round-trip at 42.583 miles per hour. The contract speed was forty miles per hour. Benjamin Foulois's account concludes, "On August 2, 1909, Aeroplane No. 1 was officially accepted into the inventory of the United States Army."

The aeronautical division of the U.S. Signal Corps had been established two years before Orville Wright's first test flight at Fort Myer. It was done without ceremony, without newspaper coverage. The stated purpose: "To study the flying machine and the possibility of adapting it to military purposes."

I wondered how much understanding anyone really could have had about what was coming. Orville, interviewed during World War I, said that he and his brother had always believed their "man-carrying" invention could prevent conflicts—surprise attacks would no longer be possible. But now, he said, America needed to build ten thousand more planes and end the war in ten weeks, even striking munitions plants inside Germany. And later he wrote:

"My brother and I thought that [the aeroplane's] use would be principally scouting in warfare, carrying mail, and other light loads to places inaccessible by rail or water, and sport. But the wildest stretch of the imagination of that time would not have permitted us to believe that . . . thousands of these machines would be in the air engaged in deadly combat. . . . We did not foresee the extent to which the aeroplane might be used in carrying the battle line to the industrial centers and into the midst of non-combatants, though we did think it might be used in dropping an occasional bomb about the heads of the rulers who declared war and stayed home."

CHAPTER SEVEN

NEW YORK HARBOR

STAND ON THE SEAWALL OF GOVERNORS ISLAND AND LOOK west to the Statue of Liberty and north to close by Manhattan, then up the Hudson River with New Jersey on the far side, and you have to think—why would Wilbur want to fly here? The river currents clash in the Atlantic's tidal flow, the winds tangle and swirl down along the New Jersey Palisades and rush out from the ranks of tall buildings—why would he take the risk?

By 1909 both of the brothers had flown for demonstration purposes, Wilbur in Europe, Orville at Fort Myer, but were disdainful of *exhibition* flying. Military trials, yes. Prizes, sometimes. Competitions, never. They didn't like the restive curiosity of the crowds, and wanted the final say on wind and flight path.

But in late summer of 1909, the brothers found reason to fly before thousands of spectators. Wilbur accepted an invitation to join the Hudson-Fulton Celebration, in New York, starting in September. The money was good—a promise of $15,000, and the Wright name would again be in the headlines of all the world's papers. Orville had left a month earlier, with Katharine, for a round of flights in Berlin, and then Potsdam. The French were already under contract with the Wrights to build planes, and now a German Wright Company would do the same, paying the brothers a 10-percent royalty in addition to a cash bonus for signing a contract. And as in France, demonstration flying and pilot training were part of the deal.

Orville decided—after a cautionary telegram from Wilbur— not to enter the year's biggest air show, out in the French countryside at Reims. Champagne companies had offered the prize money, and thus the weeklong event was the *Grande Semaine d'Aviation de la Champagne.* Three French-built Wright Flyers performed at Reims, but not impressively. The big prize was for a speed race, two timed laps around an oval course marked by red-and-white pylons. Glenn Curtiss had brought his own new plane—the *Reims Racer*—from Hammondsport, New York. It was small and light, and, with a fifty-horsepower engine, powered around the turns at 47.10 miles an hour. But Louis Blériot was the crowd's favorite. In July the Frenchman had flown his monoplane across the English Channel in twenty-three minutes, winning the *London Daily Mail* prize and enabling publisher Lord Northcliffe to warn in stentorian print, "England is no longer an island." Blériot also had a stronger engine for his plane at Reims, but—after all the racing times were computed—it was "The Star Spangled Banner" that the band played, and Glenn Curtiss was crowned the air speed king of the world.

In Berlin, Orville kept to his business, writing to his brother Lorin, who was handling the finances back in Dayton, "I am sending a draft for $40,000. If Will is not at home please place it in different building associations."

Orville made nineteen flights in Germany; some days the crowds were estimated at 200,000. Among the royal family there was great appreciation for the airplane's military potential, and the Kaiser's son, Prince Friedrich Wilhelm, went up for a fifteen-minute ride. Orville's most impressive performance was a climb to an altitude that, if officially measured, would easily break the record of 155 meters, just set at Reims. Orville said, "I never flew so high before. I estimated that I reached an altitude of 500 meters (1,697 feet). It is difficult to gauge height, but I make the estimate from the time it took me from the starting point to the greatest altitude. Immediately after rising I set the height rudder at the maximum and kept climbing steadily for fifteen minutes. The descent I made in five minutes. I came down at a simply terrifying speed. The whole machine shook as it rushed through the air."

Two hallmarks of modern aviation can be traced back to Orville's demonstrations in Germany. One evening in Potsdam he stayed up so long he was flying in the dark. Spectators turned on their automobile headlights, training them on the landing field. And Orville began thinking about seat belts: "In the early flights in winds the machine was jerked from under me a number of times, and I would find myself sitting five or six inches up the back of the seat. Saturday afternoon . . . I got caught by [a rolling gust] that raised me 8 or ten inches off the seat. As I try to hold myself in the seat by pushing myself tight against the back I rode for quite a distance before I slipped down to the seat. I am going to tie myself to the seat with string."

Once again, in the fall of 1909, the brothers were apart, flying on different continents, each reading about the other's accomplishments in the newspapers. Wilbur, living in a New York City hotel, seemed lonely, and wrote to Katharine in

Berlin: "I see you in front of the crowds with the empress and princesses, etc. and not writing any letters, but all right for you. Just wait till winter comes and then you'll get the bad of it just like any other grasshopper after the festive summer season is over. I have had *one* letter since you left home more than six weeks ago. There may have been two but it has been so long ago that I cannot remember clearly any more."

When I first read about the Hudson-Fulton events in New York in 1909, I got out the maps. How, I wondered, would I get to Governors Island? The answer involved Renée Miscione of the U.S. General Services Administration and a friendly tugboat crew.

"These are my buddies," Renée says, as they give us a hand over the bow rail of the sturdy white tug called the *Swivel*. They slip the loops of thick rope off the dock pilings, and the boat backs out of the ornate old copper-green ferry terminal and into the East River, toward Brooklyn. Governors Island is straight ahead, a half-mile away, just a bit southeast off the tip of Manhattan.

Wilbur Wright made startling flights that are now mostly forgotten from this New York City island that many people don't even know is here. On the maps it tends to get lost—it's frequently unlabeled—in the jumble of more significant landmarks at the bottom of Manhattan. There's no public access, and because of the island's long military history, there never has been. The Coast Guard ran a large operation here for thirty years and still has some caretaking chores, but Governors Island is historically a domain of the U.S. Army, which took it over from British forces, who had displaced the Dutch, who bought the land from the Manhatas Indians in 1637 for two ax handles, a string of beads, and a handful of nails. The GSA administers the island for the government, and, according to Renée, between fifty and sixty people work here today, mostly GSA security, the fire station crew, and coast guard personnel. (In April 2003, New York's governor, George Pataki, gave President George Bush a one-dollar bill, buying the island for the state. The plan is to establish a new City University of New York campus; the historic district will remain under National Park Service jurisdiction.)

Renée and I stand on the *Swivel*'s deck, in a good breeze, bracing as the tug pushes through a chop left behind by the morning's storm. "This crew runs back and forth all day, taking workers across, delivering stuff."

I ask, "Anyone living on the island now?"

"No, not since the base closed."

Renée's staff has a van waiting for us at the island ferry landing, and she takes me for a slow, conversation-filled drive, past the home of the New York colony's British governor, past Castle Williams, built of red sandstone as a circular fort, which was used during the Civil War as a prison for Confederate soldiers and troops, and later as an army stockade. "They're pretty sure that Walt Disney was in there for being absent without leave," Renée says, "And Rocky Graziano, you know, the boxer, for the same thing. And Dick and Tommy Smothers were born at the base hospital; their dad was stationed here."

We walk the ramparts of Fort Jay, which is star-shaped, with a dry moat. The massive black cannons are still in place. "Those are fifteen-inch and ten-inch guns, dating back to 1861. We've been told that with the right trajectory you could fire a shell all the way up to Central Park, but that's not a certified fact."

Next the vast red-brick sprawl of Building 400, a barracks reaching almost all the way across the island, built, Renée says, by the army to prevent Mayor Fiorello La Guardia, who'd been a World War I pilot, from putting an airport here.

I ask Renée for time alone, to walk along the western seawall. The tide is high, the waters of the Upper Bay barely a foot below the roadway, and a wave comes pouring over to catch my shoes and pants. The Staten Island ferry goes cruising past, orange against the gray-blue water and sky.

Across the way I can see the Statue of Liberty and Ellis Island. To the north, the expanse of the Hudson River, the silver and black stacks of Wall Street office towers. I walk on around the western turn of the island and find the thin strandwork of the Brooklyn Bridge, high above the East River. In 1909 the buildings would have been of lesser scale, but all that I am seeing now would have been within Wilbur's view. He stood here on the grass by the seawall, trying to determine the action of the wind and guess at an altitude that might work. Wilbur's $15,000 contract was simple and not especially daunting. He'd promised to make one flight, either for ten miles or lasting for one hour. But the Statue of Liberty seems close, and Grant's Tomb is not that far away on the Hudson, and *just perhaps* it would be feasible to fly up the East River and across to the Hudson and back down—a circumnavigation of Manhattan.

All the routes would be mostly over water, and Wilbur determined he needed an emergency flotation device. He bought a red canoe in the city, at the H&D Folsom Arms Company, brought it over on the ferry, fitted it up with a white canvas cover, and lashed it to the underside of his plane. The idea, in the unlikely event of a water landing, was to gain time, waiting for a rescue boat.

✦   ✦

Governors Island is shaped like an ice cream cone, with the rounded top pointing up the East River. The northern part, with the prison and the fort and the officers' houses, used to be the entire island. The southern section is landfill, sand and rock and soil hauled over from the Lexington Avenue subway excavation and used to create new parade and drill grounds. Today there are soccer and baseball fields on the filled-in part of the island, and empty family units. The coast guard motor pool was here, and a buoy repair shop, plus Lima and Tango and Yankee Piers, reaching out into Buttermilk Channel, between the island and Brooklyn.

The photographs from 1909 show a gritty, grass-sparse plain with vague, distant buildings across the water views. The Hudson-Fulton organizers must have thought Governors Island was a great place to fly from. They could use the soldiers to help out, and let just important people and the press ride over on the ferry. Also, the symbolism was stunning. Three hundred years earlier the English navigator Henry Hudson left Amsterdam in April in a small ship, the *Half Moon,* and, in September 1609, in search of a northwest passage to the Pacific, discovered the route through the narrows and sailed past the site of Governors Island on his way up the tidal estuary to Albany. Two hundred years later, in August of 1807, steaming to Albany one day and back to New York the next, Robert Fulton opened a new era of travel with his paddlewheel *Clermont.*

SAYS HE COULD FLY OVER SKYSCRAPERS

Hudson-Fulton was a two week extravaganza, with military parades, concerts, speeches and fireworks. City Hall, the

Washington Square Arch, even the towers and spans of the Brooklyn Bridge were outlined against a dark sky by thousands of lights powered by the new technology of electricity. *Harper's Weekly* captioned their set of photographs GLEAMS FROM NEW YORK'S SPECTACULAR NIGHT.

Many nations had sent their warships to be part of the festive flotilla on the Hudson. Among the vessels were the *Drake* and the *Argyll,* from Britain. The German cruiser *Bremen.* Italy sent the cruisers *Aetna* and *Etruria.* From France, the *Liberté* and the *Vérité.* The flagship *Connecticut* represented the United States. Replicas of Hudson's *Half Moon* and Fulton's *Clermont* were also on the water, and *Harper's* headlined the scene, THE TINY CRAFT AND THEIR PONDEROUS DESCENDANTS.

Sailing vessels, steamboats, and waterways, and now—the airplane. A new century was under way, and it was time the people of New York City saw someone fly. Glenn Curtiss had also been invited, but the performance his contract called for was more challenging than Wilbur Wright's. Curtiss was to fly ten miles up the Hudson and ten miles back, making a turn at Grant's Tomb. And because he'd made his deal before his triumph at Reims, Curtiss was flying for less money, just $5,000.

Two airplane hangars had been built at the edge of the Governors Island field. Wilbur and mechanic Charlie Taylor started their uncrating and assembly on September 20. On the twenty-first, Curtiss, just returning from France, docked in New York. On the morning of the twenty-second he came to Governors Island to see about preparations. He had a brief, apparently cordial talk with Wilbur, who had no doubt seen Curtiss's photograph on the cover of *Harper's Weekly* and asked about the flying at Reims. The next day Curtiss took the train upstate to Hammondsport, where he received a hometown hero's welcome, and didn't return to Governors Island until the twenty-eighth.

Curtiss's now famous *Reims Racer* never made it to Governors Island, because for a $5,000 promotional fee he had promised the plane to Wanamaker's department store upon its immediate return from Europe. So for the Hudson-Fulton exhibition he would use a different aircraft, as yet untested, that had only half the horsepower of his champion *Racer.*

Alexander Mason, a reporter for the *New York Herald,* became fascinated by the differences between the two men who were preparing to honor their innovative forebears Hudson and Fulton by flying an airplane over New York City for the first time ever. He wrote first about Wilbur's hangar: "It is the cage of the Wright biplane and in it the white flyer has grown from the infancy of packing boxes into a full-fledged airship under the hands of a man who has evidently forgotten how to talk, a man who seems to have no desire to make friends. This man Wright is interesting in the extreme; you know he is unusual the instant you see him."

As a reporter trying to write a feature story, Mason would have settled for only a few comments from Wilbur Wright, something to be able to quote. But his description of Wright at work is surely more revealing than an interview. Mason's prose matches what you can now see in photographs from Governors Island:

As he has worked over his biplane many have watched the deft fingers which make no useless moves, the keen gray eyes which glance from wing to wing with frightening rapidity or settle intently upon the whirring motor. He is . . . thin, supple, graceful, quick upon his feet and evidently quicker still of thought. He has worked here in his shirt-sleeves, sans overalls or apron— you cannot think of him in such togs or with spots of grease or dabs of oil upon him. With him has worked an equally taciturn mechanician, a man who seems to understand the every thought of Wright and to antici-pate his every wish as well as the every need of the strange machine which they have brought to life.

Mason found a more encouraging welcome in the Curtiss camp:

In the other little shed is a far different group of men, a much smaller and much better finished machine bird. Glenn H. Curtiss is the antithesis of Wilbur Wright. One hates to talk, the other loves it. Like Wright, Curtiss is tall and slender, but his face is not so striking nor as strong. He is a good six feet tall and can't add much over 150 pounds to the load of his little air-ship. . . . Curtiss is more than an inventor, he is the fore-runner of the type who will take up real aeronautics within the next year, young men who like different and dangerous things because they are difficult and danger-ous. He does not putter over his plane; he has brought men down from his upstate factory to do that for him. The Curtiss biplane is much like the Wright in many ways, only it's very much smaller and is a beautiful piece of finished workmanship. Its size is the first thing that impresses you after you have left the big white plane nearby. The Curtiss machine doesn't look half as large. It is brown, dark brown on the wings, the golden brown of highly varnished bamboo on the supports.

One of the first Hudson-Fulton headlines to appear proved presumptive:

CURTISS RISES LIKE BIRD

On the twenty-ninth, Glenn Curtiss, who had slept in his hangar, took off at 7:00 A.M. for a brief flight around the island. He had trouble with the wind, and the plane's wheels proved awkward in the sand. High winds for several days kept his plane grounded. He made one more short flight into the turbulence over the river, then landed, and the next day crated up his airplane—he was due for an appearance in St. Louis. It would be Wilbur Wright's flying at the Hudson-Fulton Celebration that thrilled a million spectators in New York and the readers of hundreds of newspapers around the country and the world.

Wilbur began with a test flight. He wanted to see how the canoe tied under his lower wing might affect the plane's handling, so he lifted off for a seven-minute run out over Buttermilk Channel. Then the moment came when the reporters knew they had a real story:

LIBERTY STATUE ENCIRCLED BY WRIGHT IN AEROPLANE

A wireless radio message went out from the island, transmitted by another great inventor, Guglielmo Marconi, who, in

1895 in Bologna, Italy, had sent the first radio signal via electro-magnetic waves. Now, in response to Marconi's alert, signal flags were raised on the ships at anchor and above downtown sky-scrapers. Wilbur was ready for his first flight, to Bedloe's Island.

From a newspaper account:

> A soft, steady breeze came from the west. Directly into this the aeroplane, which is silver in color, left the monorail, at 10:18:04 o'clock. Straight almost as an arrow the wings of Wilbur flew to the Statue of Liberty, a mile and a quarter away. . . . Suddenly there appeared beyond the curve of Castle Williams, the bow of the *Lusitania,* bound for Liverpool. It was as if she had risen from the sea to give contrast to the scene. Her decks were fringed white with flying handkerchiefs; a cheer that was faint came floating across the water. . . . an Irishman who was present said, "Wright is now where the hand of man has never set a foot."

Another headline writer mildly overstated the feat:

COULD HAVE TOUCHED GODDESS'S HAND

It was a six-and-a-half minute flight. Wilbur estimated his speed at just over fifty miles an hour, and told a reporter after-ward that he felt his plane "rock and reel" as he passed above the burst of steam from the *Lusitania*'s saluting whistle. Wilbur Wright's flying on this morning from Governors Island in New York Harbor was the first ever over American waters.

At noon Wilbur took the ferry across to Manhattan for a luncheon at the Singer Tower, then the tallest building in the world. From the fortieth-floor observatory, he had an aviator's view of the city, but he was not so much searching for a landing site as trying to figure out where turbulence might arise. Glenn Curtiss had said earlier, "I wouldn't fly over the buildings of the city if they deeded to me everything that I passed over."

Renée Miscione calls the *Swivel*'s captain on her cell phone, and soon the tugboat has us back across the East River at the ferry terminal. On Renée's parting recommendation, I walk two blocks west to see the Cass Gilbert–designed United States Custom House, which she told me was completed in 1907 and so was brand-new at the time of the Hudson-Fulton Celebration. "I'm sure Wilbur admired it," she said.

A metal-banging cab ride up the West Side Highway delivers me to Grant's Tomb in Riverside Park at 122nd Street in less than fifteen minutes. Today there are golden sycamores and London plane trees along the walkway that leads to the tomb entrance. An American flag flies to the left of the entrance, and Ulysses S. Grant's general's flag, red with four white stars, to the right. The granite structure reflects white in the sun, and it's still a landmark, even though the Riverside Church is now a much taller presence just across the street. When Wilbur flew this way in 1909, he would have seen the tomb standing alone, austere, at the highest point on the east side of the river.

Wilbur's contract called for a long flight, so why not take over Glenn Curtiss's mission to Grant's Tomb and have the thing done? He took off at 9:53 on Monday morning, flying with a life jacket, the canoe, and three small American flags attached to his plane. Ten miles up the Hudson in twenty minutes, over the array of battleships and ferryboats and yachts. Again he noticed turbulence from the steam whistles, and now the side-draft deflections from the Manhattan streets. Once he dipped to within fifteen feet of the water before rising again, but he was 150 feet above the British warship *Drake* as he made the turn just beyond Grant's Tomb. Up the river and back: thirty-three minutes, thirty-three seconds.

OVER THE BIG SHIPS THE MAN–BIRD FLEW

AEROPLANIST PLEASED WITH THE BEHAVIOR OF THE MACHINE

A poet, Percy McKaye, was standing in lower Manhattan's Battery Park that morning of October 4, a witness to Wilbur's take-off and safe return. Inspired by the flight, he wrote a poem called "The Air Voyage up the Hudson," which includes these stanzas:

> *We caught our breath, as we watched him bound*
> *Where the air-billow swirls and serries,*
> *And the shout of our straining hearts is drowned*
> *In the din of the roaring ferries.*
>
> *He has flashed; he is gone; only fancy aids*
> *Our eyes where the haze grows hoarer:*
> *The Ages look up from the Palisades,*
> *That looked down on the Dutch explorer.*
>
> *But what of their dreams—those gray steel hulks*
> *Deep-moored in the river below him,*

With the loins of a nation girt in their bulks?
In their iron hearts, do they know him?

Do their deadly engines twinge with a doubt,
A dread of this thing ethereal,
That hides in its plumes the earliest scout
Of the armies and navies aerial?

And what of their hearts—that human throng?
Do they hail in the creature regal
The harbinger of dirge, or of song?
A vulture, or an eagle?

He tacks; he returns; the news is blown
On the winds of a city's wonder:
He comes, in the braying megaphone,
He comes, on Manhattan's thunder;

He looms once more by the swarming bluffs—
A bird of marshes gigantic—
And slants on the slumbering mist, and luffs
To his nest by the booming Atlantic.

Back on Governors Island, in the afternoon of the same day, Wilbur and Charlie Taylor started getting the plane set up for another trip, possibly a complete circuit of Manhattan. They were turning the propellers to crank the engine when a cylinder head exploded, ruining the engine and ripping a gash in the top wing. Wilbur told reporters, "No more flights in New York."

The next day he left by train for Washington, D.C., to set up a new army flight school at nearby College Park, Maryland, using the same plane that Orville had flown at Fort Myer. Wilbur's last public flights came during the month he spent at College Park. One of his passengers was Sarah Van Deman, the wife of a Signal Corps officer. She went flying with Wilbur on October 27, and earned this headline in the Washington *Evening Star*:

WOMAN TRIES FLYING. FIRST OF HER SEX
IN THE UNITED STATES TO HAVE THE PRIVILEGE

The *Star* noted, "It was only after Mrs. Van Deman had obtained permission from her husband that Mr. Wright consented to take her for a flight," and that she was in the air for a total of fifteen minutes.

Before leaving New York, and my own train ride to Washington, D.C., I spent an hour on a bench under the trees at Grant's Tomb, looking out over the Hudson, imagining the fleet of ships and the noise and the crowd looking far down the river to see the small white biplane approach.

It is difficult to find firsthand accounts from the New Yorkers who watched Wilbur's flights from Governors Island. A century later it is almost impossible to understand what an airplane might have meant to someone seeing it for the first time.

This description helps; it's from a newspaper: "The sight took your breath away. It was all so new, all so totally different, and more thrilling than one thought it was going to be. There is nothing else like it. It is worth going far to see. It must be worth going half around the world to try."

CHAPTER EIGHT

THE OSHKOSH AIR SHOW

I T WAS IN LATE JULY WHEN I DROVE NORTH TO SEE THE AIR-planes. There was a shimmer of humidity over the soybean fields and the corn, through Ohio, Indiana, then Illinois and Wisconsin. I took the state roads when I could, stopped in small-town cafes when I could find them, and people would say, "Oshkosh? Oh, yeah, I've always wanted to go up there. There've been planes passing over here for a couple of days now, heading up to the fly-in."

Along the way I took time out to see a man about bicycles, to ask about their importance in the development of the Wright brothers as airplane builders and pilots. Richard Schwinn walked me through his high-end bike factory, where he makes Waterford Precision Cycles, named after his southeastern Wisconsin town. His bikes are handcrafted from state-of-the art steel tubing, and they're expensive. That description also fits the bikes the Wrights were producing in the 1890s.

Sitting across a table in his factory's coffee room, Richard says, "A really famous brand bike in those days could cost—in terms of today's money—more than three thousand dollars. There was an absolute craze going on and it lasted for about ten years. This was after the safety bicycle was invented and you didn't have that dangerous high front wheel anymore. These new bikes were lightweight and easy to ride and liberating. For the first time a man and woman could go out unchaperoned, a young woman could go sailing down a country road with her hair flying in the breeze, a worker could get to his factory job and ride home for lunch. And it was a super-dynamic opportunity for a young engineer."

It was Richard Schwinn's great-grandfather Ignaz who helped America make the transition from the horse-and buggy to the automobile. Ignaz—who'd apprenticed in a piano factory—had come from Germany to see the 1893 Chicago World's Fair. Fascinated by this country and the spirit for innovation he found here, he never left and soon became one of Chicago's three hundred bike manufacturers.

Wilbur and Orville (who conceivably could have walked past Ignaz Schwinn along the Chicago exposition's midway) opened their first bike shop at about the same time. They'd both owned bikes, and Orville had won prizes for racing. At the Wright Cycle Exchange on West Third Street in Dayton they did repairs and sold several brands. Later they designed and built their own, with the best one, the Van Cleve, selling for forty-seven dollars (about $1,000 today). The brothers applied much of their fabrication training and many of their bicycle parts to their planes—chains, sprockets, hubs—and you can easily spot the basic bike frame triangle in the structure of some of the Wright Flyers. And Wilbur's understanding of how an airplane must bank and turn came directly from his study of the bicycle. He had observed that when riders turned to the left they began with a slight counter-steer, "turning the handlebar to the right, and then as the machine inclined to the left, they turned the handlebar to the left and as a result made the circle, inclining inwardly."

Back on the road to the Oshkosh fly-in convention, I kept thinking of Wilbur and Orville and how they might have enjoyed such a gathering. The Wrights didn't have many friends in aviation; they did have competitors, and they'd made enemies of many of those. A 1910 patent suit victory and a court injunction gave the brothers the right to collect royalties from practically anyone or any company making money with airplanes.

It had been a lonely business anyway. How would you know about somebody trying to put a plane together by lantern light in a barn twenty miles out a country road from Indianapolis? How would you confirm if it was truth or rumor that a mechanic in New Jersey might have a nifty engine he was just about ready to test? And after their many hours in the air, whom could the Wrights talk with about flying, about the fearful balance at the edge of a stall? However, despite their reputation for fiercely protecting their patents, Oshkosh honors Wilbur and Orville as colleagues, as theoretical founding members, as the original aircraft homebuilders, as the first test pilots.

Oshkosh is a city on the western shore of a large lake— Winnebago—which is roughly halfway between Milwaukee, to the southeast, and Green Bay, to the northeast. Highway traffic starts slowing ten miles outside of Oshkosh, and arriving aircraft are assigned landing times while they are still several states away. Vacationing FAA controllers, selected from among the best in their regions, come each year to help out in the five-story brick structure from which hangs a banner that says WORLD'S BUSIEST CONTROL TOWER.

This summer's event is the fiftieth annual gathering of the Experimental Aircraft Association, and is known formally as EAA AirVenture Oshkosh 2002. Paul and Audrey Poberezny started the EAA in the basement of their Milwaukee home. They were married in Arkansas, where he was a flight instructor for the U.S. Army. The first fly-in convention attracted the old standards like a Waco, a Stearman, a Curtiss Jenny, plus planes that people built at home from *Mechanix Illustrated* plans or original, one-of-a-kind designs that they developed themselves. There was the *Knight Twister,* a plane called the *Yellow Jacket,* a *Belly Flopper,* a *Tater Chip,* one named the *Rose Parakeet.*

Paul Poberezny, waiting at the airfield that first year, wasn't sure who might show up. Later he said, "I was looking to the south, waiting for the homebuilts to come. I saw the specks in the sky, and it was the greatest thrill for me. . . . I greeted everybody. Parked everybody. Got on the phone—a nickel a call—to find everybody a place to stay. Like a whirlwind. No elaborate planning, but the enthusiasm was there."

By 2002 the numbers had exploded: 10,000 aircraft, 5,000 volunteers, 750 exhibitors, and 750,000 visitors in attendance over the seven-day event. Watch planes, talk planes, sell planes, buy planes. Listen to a lecture on "Computational Fluid Dynamics" or "Rust Prevention" or "Aluminum Forming" or "TIG Welding" or "Flying for Peace, India to Laos, in a Zenair

CH 701." Get General Chuck Yeager's autograph and meet the astronauts Gene Cernan and James Lovell, or Dick Rutan, co-pilot of the *Voyager,* the first plane to fly nonstop around the world—nine days in 1986. If you own and fly an airplane, a Cessna 172, a Piper Dakota, a Mooney, you needn't worry that the motels are jammed for seventy miles around; just fly here, tie down on a grassy field, put up a tent, and go look for friends from last summer.

At Oshkosh the ultralight people have a separate campground and their own flying space; at dusk you can see swarms of the tiny craft climbing in spirals, almost transparent in the south-western sky. And in a nearby cove of Lake Winnebago, one hundred seaplanes, more than a third of them from Canada, lie at rest, secured to moorings.

The size of Oshkosh is best appreciated from above, and I was pleased to learn that the EAA was taking people up in their restored Ford Tri-Motor. A shuttle bus carried us out to one of the quieter airstrips where the Tri-Motor was waiting. The plane has three engines, huge for their time, one in front and one tucked under each wing. The fuselage is made from corrugated aluminum. It's a tail-dragger, sitting back at a severe angle.

One of the two young pilots helps us climb in. There are nine seats in all, one on each side of the center aisle. The interior is pale green metal and mahogany. The windows are large, and we have a view forward into the raised cockpit area.

The engines are cranked. One starts, the second, then the third adds a note that blends into a metallic growl. We start a slow roll over the grass and sweep around onto the pavement, and, after a pause, a full-power takeoff run as the Ford Tri-Motor almost jumps into the air.

These planes were America's first airliners. The experience had to be scary, had to be loud, might have made you airsick, but you wouldn't ever forget the flight. This particular Tri-Motor, serial number 69, had its maiden flight seventy years ago, and in 1930 it inaugurated Cubana Airlines' route between Havana and Santiago de Cuba.

We bank out over the lake and head north, past downtown Oshkosh and on to Neenah, ten miles away, then a tight turn west, then south, and we're on approach for Wittman Regional Airport and the vista that is Oshkosh. The lake and farmland, then the airport terminal with taxiways leading out to parallel runways. On the west side of the airstrips are the office buildings and hangars and exhibit halls of the Experimental Aircraft Association—and airplanes by the thousands, parked together by types: World War II fighters, Stearmans, Bonanzas. Plus ranks of trucks, camper vans, and acres and acres of cars.

There's an air show every afternoon during the fly-in at Oshkosh, and today's is under way as our shuttle bus returns to the main exhibit area. P-51 Mustangs that flew fighter escort for Allied bombers over Germany are now ripping overhead at low altitude. The noise is like the high-speed *brraat* of a model airplane, but amped up with a bass boost and spiky pops in the treble. The PA announcer says, "The P-51 is the most aerodynamically perfect pursuit plane in existence. Fifteen thousand of these planes were made, only sixty of them are flying today. After the war you could have picked up one for six hundred to twelve hundred dollars. Right now the bigger side of one million dollars will get you into the airplane."

I find quiet, shade, and lunch inside a food pavilion and take some time to look through the EAA's program. The word EXPERIMENTAL appears throughout its pages. Because I liked the typography—black lettering on clear film—I've bought an EXPERIMENTAL sticker; it's the same one you see on the more unusual aircraft.

After lunch I ask Steve Nusbaum if he'll explain it for me. He has an exhibit nearby, with a lemon-yellow fabric-covered plane he's built and is offering for sale as a kit.

"You've got a fifty-one-percent rule from the Federal Aviation Administration. They have a checklist for any home-builder to determine the way his aircraft was constructed. Does the homebuilder do the fabric work? Does he do the welding? Then he gets checks in his column. But if a factory builds the engine or machines a part, then the checks go in the factory's column. You add up the two columns, and as long as the home-builder comes up with more points than the manufacturer, his plane qualifies as a homebuilt, experimental aircraft."

"And that's good or bad?" I ask.

"That's good because then the builder becomes the manufac-turer and is eligible to do all the maintenance rather than take it to a shop where the work has to be certified by the FAA, which means big bucks."

"So you're proud to have an EXPERIMENTAL sticker?"

"You bet."

Steve Nusbaum is from Hebron, Illinois, just down over the line from Wisconsin. He's retired from a factory job making brake parts, but he'd always had a touch for fixing planes and fly-ing them. As a kid he'd ride his bike out to the airfield and spend hours with the guys at the maintenance hangar.

"This plane you see here represents eight years of research and development out of my own pocket. It's hard to find investors to fork over a lot of money for something as scary as flying airplanes, particularly these unusual ones."

Steve's experimental is called the *John Doe*—his frustrated response to a neighbor's questions about a name. It comes in a $19,500 kit. The engine he recommends, from a Czech Republic company, costs $12,000 more. After four hundred hours of labor, you could paint it any color you wanted, taxi out to the runway, and scoot up into the air, knowing you were the very first person to fly *this* plane.

"Who's the customer, what's special here?" I ask.

Nusbaum replies, "You're going to see this plane in Alaska, in the Australian Outback, down in South Africa. It's designed for bush pilots, or pipeline work or state forestry people. It's got an extremely short takeoff, 120 feet, and it lands in 120 feet. Plus it's field repairable. You carry tools and spare parts and if you crash into a tree and rip off an elevator, you can fix it. You can put in a new aluminum strut without taking the wing off. Sew on some new fabric and you're good to fly."

The aerial stage, the sky at Oshkosh, is wide and high and today is a sparkling blue. The main runways are laid out in a straight north-south direction, so the spectators, all on the west side, are looking east, with the sun behind them. The pilots, flying north or south, avoid the glare as well.

The show opens each day with skydivers drifting down, one carrying a giant American flag, making gentle turns in the air to land just at the moment the national anthem ends on the PA.

The World War II Warbirds blast through their performance. Bob and Pat Wagner go up in their Waco (pronounced WAH-koh) biplane. Bob does the flying and Pat is standing on the top wing. She's excited, waving her arms as the plane dives and even rolls over, and from a distance you don't even notice the careful rigging that holds her on. The Wagners, long married, have been doing their wing-walking act for thirty years.

Four red-and-white Stearman biplanes come in low from the left, over the trees, then rise and spin off and soar up in different directions. These are the Red Barons. An article in the Oshkosh newspaper says, "The squadron, which promotes a brand of pizza, is named after World War I flying ace Baron Manfred von Richthofen."

I've been waiting to see Patty Wagstaff. I've read her autobiography, *Fire and Air: A Life on the Edge.* She was born in 1951, daughter of an air force pilot. Her first flying was in Alaska with a boyfriend who owned a Cessna 185 floatplane. She soloed in 1980, took aerobatic instruction in 1982, learning about loops and rolls and tail slides, and in 1991, '92, and '93 she won the National Aerobatic Championship.

"Smoke's on," Patty's announcer says, and the crowd locates her gleaming red-and-white plane, a stream of white spilling into the sky as she climbs even higher.

Aerobatics is most usefully defined in the book *Basic Aerobatics* as "an intentional departure from straight and level flight to fly one maneuver or a series of premeditated maneuvers that require extremes of bank, pitch, and acceleration." Aerobatic pilots practice and perform inside a box of air. It's as if they can see the lines of a square that floats steady above the runway. The box is about three thousand feet wide, deep, and high, and in a competition the judges are stationed at various key spots on the field, and they radio in any transgressions. On air show days, Patty Wagstaff enters a space she can only imagine, and before a crowd she cannot hear she attempts to fly a routine that is, she hopes, "as fiery and gyrating as that of a flamenco dancer." Her plane is handbuilt in Germany by Walter Extra. He calls it the Extra 300S. The engine is a Lycoming, rated at 330 horsepower. Patty sits under a canopy in her cockpit just back of the wing.

As she performs, her announcer describes what she's doing, but I don't listen, and the PA techno-rock music seems to fade into stillness. I am only aware of the motor's changing pitch and volume as the Extra flashes by almost at eye level and then *snaps* straight up, a vertical climb at full power, yet the plane is spinning slowly as it rises. The climb slows, then stops. For the time of a breath, Patty's plane is motionless in the air two thousand feet high. A long curl of white smoke feathers out below. Then the Extra slides back, holding its vertical position, tail down, falling off to the side, powering into a dive, the wings hesitating at one angle, then quickly rolling to another.

Some of these maneuvers evolved from the evasion-and-attack techniques developed by the first combat pilots in Europe. And the standard aerobatic figures have names like Immelmann, Avalanche, Humpty Bump, Hammerhead, and Reverse Half Cuban Eight. Patty's closing stunt is not one of the classics; it's contemporary, seldom performed, and perfectly described by its name: the Inverted Ribbon Cut.

We hear, but do not yet see, the Extra 300S rocketing in from the right. Two men stand on either side of the runway, each holding a pole with a white string stretched between. A length of bright orange surveyor's tape flutters at the center of the string. Suddenly Patty flashes through *upside down* and rips past, exploding the string and tape in a burst of color, then climbs, still upside down. The string was held taut at twenty-two feet above the runway, and Patty cut it with the tail of her plane.

I thought about this ribbon cut for several months afterward; it kept playing in my mind. And in the winter I phoned Patty's headquarters in Florida to ask how she learned to do such a thing.

She started with slow upside-down passes. Then the string was set up, high at first, then lower and lower for her practice runs. She said, "I remember lying in bed thinking that was the weirdest thing I've ever done. There's something about low flying that's great, and it's even cooler to be upside down. You line up with the edge of the runway and try to spot the string."

I asked Patty about the adrenaline rush, flying fast and upside down. "People think what I do is about the thrill of it, and some people even suspect there's a sexual sensation. If I feel adrenaline it means something's not right. I can be on the ground looking at the airplane on the ramp and just sense it. Nothing sexual either, although we do joke that you can tell by how someone flies how they might be in bed. You can recognize a pilot's flying even if they're in a different plane—some are jerky, some are smooth, the personality comes out."

At the end of Patty's autobiography there's a list of sixty-four names of close friends who have died. Five of the names have an asterisk, and a footnote explains: "People with an asterisk beside their name did not die in an aviation accident." Patty believes the number of aviation deaths among people she's known has probably doubled since that list was published in 1997. She told me, "My attitude is that we're not here very long, and I guess that indicates a certain philosophy. What I'm doing with flying gives me a freedom that makes life worthwhile. I think I'm good with death issues; I can cope with it. I've thought of volunteering for hospice work."

✢   ✢

In April of 1917, Orville Wright was featured in a *Harper's Weekly* article titled "The Safe and Useful Aeroplane." Orville told the interviewer:

> Certain performers have done much to instill this notion that flying is exceedingly dangerous. These are the daredevil exhibition flyers, who cultivate the circus aspects of the art. Both by words and deeds they have associated the aeroplane with the idea of danger. They have spread abroad the impression that only an immense amount of nerve, abnormal skill, and plenty of luck qualify one for aviation. And their air acrobatics—their tail glides and their loopings-the-loop—have accentuated this idea. . . . Yet I do not wish to criticize too harshly these circus-performers, for they have accomplished much good. The man who first looped-the-loop made a solid contribution to the cause of aeronautics, for he demonstrated the wonderful stability and righting-power of the aeroplane. What other means of transportation, except the aeroplane, sails just as well upside down?

Orville was speaking from a dispassionate distance in 1917; seven years before this interview the Wright brothers had themselves entered the exhibition flying business. They hired and trained nine pilots; it would prove to be an extremely dangerous occupation.

Early in 1910 the American Wright Company in Dayton was building two airplanes a month. Attendance was enthusiastic at air shows around the country. The brothers decided to put planes and pilots together and make some money. Orville went to Montgomery, Alabama, to set up a flying school on land that formerly was a cotton plantation. Wilbur had picked out the site during a tour of the South, looking for warmer conditions than Huffman Prairie offered in March.

A flying machine arrived, seven crates in the train baggage car. Charlie Taylor came with his toolbox, and Orville followed five days later. The first airplane over Montgomery was seen on March 26, with the newspaper noting, "Under perfect control it followed the hand of Orville Wright turning, descending at his bidding."

Three young men left Montgomery as successful pilot trainees: A. L. Welsh of Washington, D.C., who'd been at Fort Myer when Orville flew, Walter Brookins, a former student of Katharine's at Dayton's Steele High, and an automobile racer and mechanic from California named Arch Hoxsey. They stand in the front line of a hangar photo taken with Orville: Welsh, leaning on a sawhorse, tie tucked in his shirt, Brookins, in a vest and bow tie, left hip cocked, and the taller, blond Hoxsey, wearing glasses, hands in his pockets. As they look toward the camera they exude confidence. It's the spring of 1910, and soon they will be the best at what they do.

One moonlit, cloudless night at Montgomery, Walter Brookins and Arch Hoxsey took the plane out at 10:30 P.M. and made several flights. Orville had already left for Dayton, and Brookins was teaching Hoxsey, who was soon to solo. They both flew that night in Alabama, and the newspaper later reported: "A dark, weird, uncertain bulk, glinting now and then in the moonlight as its burnished bars caught the rays, and spouting sparks in mid-air, the aeroplane of the Wright brothers was driven in what is believed to have been the first flight by night ever attempted."

By the end of May, all the training had been shifted to Huffman Prairie. Six more pilots qualified, including Ralph

Johnstone of Kansas City, who'd been performing as a trick bicycle rider. In their first exhibition outing, in Indianapolis, the Wright team did some ordinary flying around the Indianapolis Motor Speedway, and Walter Brookins climbed past six thousand feet to set a record, but the promoters had wanted something more exciting.

Glenn Curtiss had his own team of pilots out on the exhibition circuit, led by the audacious Charles Hamilton, whose air show business career began on the county fair circuit—he would jump from a hot-air balloon high above, open a parachute, slow down, cut that parachute away, free-fall, then open another one. While flying for Curtiss, Hamilton was known for his scores of crashes and broken bones. His teammate Lincoln Beachey once remarked, "There is little left of the original Hamilton." Beachey, whom Orville Wright once called the greatest flyer he'd ever seen, went on to become a high-paid solo performer. He grew arrogant, ever more reckless, contemptuous of spectators who were thrilled by the prospect of a crash, calling them "a pack of jackals, eager to be in on the kill." In 1915, Lincoln Beachey, with thousands watching, went into a steep, high-speed, fatal dive toward the waters of San Francisco Bay. The wings of his Curtiss aircraft folded back, tore off. Beachey was twenty-eight years old. Charles Hamilton, his former colleague, had died in bed of tuberculosis a year earlier, at age twenty-nine.

The Wright exhibition team, in the summer of 1910, moved on from Indianapolis to Montreal, then Atlantic City, where Walter Brookins crashed deliberately, avoiding a group of photographers who had rushed to where he was about to land. Arch

Hoxsey, flying low at the Wisconsin State Fair, injured several spectators when he lost control and landed on the wrong side of the racetrack fence.

Hoxsey and Ralph Johnstone had become known on the flying circuit as the Stardust Twins. And Johnstone developed the Dive of Death. Watching from the grandstand you'd be convinced that Johnstone had made a terrible miscalculation—the dive was too fast, far too steep, and he could never pull up in time. Wilbur Wright, in Dayton, concerned about the accidents and the risk-taking, wrote to Hoxsey and Johnstone about an exhibition coming up in Detroit: "I am very much in earnest when I say that I want no stunts and spectacular frills put on the flights there. If each of you can make a plain flight of ten to fifteen minutes each day keeping always within the inner fence wall away from the grandstand and never more than three hundred feet high it will be just what we want. Under no circumstances make more than one flight each day apiece. Anything beyond plain flying will be chalked up as a fault and not as a credit."

But think of it all from a young aviator's point of view. For example, here's a grand air meet —the International Aviation Tournament—in October 1910 at New York's Belmont Park, a horse-racing track on Long Island. You're on the Wrights' flying team, four of you are there, plus Wilbur, Orville, and Katharine, visiting from Dayton. Four pilots from the Curtiss team are entered. Nine pilots from France, three from England. And John Moisant, the Chicago architect who learned to fly in France.

The airplanes—as if they were thoroughbred horses—are kept in wooden hangars with white painted signboards: OGILVIE, AUDEMARS, GARROS, LATHAM, BALDWIN, GRAHAME-WHITE, and the others. Journalists and photographers are prepared to glorify the fearless men, and one woman, who will speed these machines into the air, and prize money is waiting in the amount of $72,300. If you are Ralph Johnstone, a pilot for Wilbur and Orville, you will assess the quality of the competition, perhaps notice the gaze of the well-dressed ladies in the grandstand, and understand that once in the air you are alone, with time and history waiting.

On October 31, Johnstone set a world's altitude record at Belmont Park. He was in a new Wright machine he called the "light roadster," and he reached 9,714 feet.

Johnstone wrote a first-hand account for the *New York American*:

Although I was in somewhat of a purple haze up there, I never lost sight of the earth. Way down below I could see trees and houses that looked smaller than toy blocks. Far over to one side I could get a fleeting glimpse of the ocean. As a guidepost, I kept a narrow, ribbon-like road running north and south. Like everything else, the road looked "dished" below me.

Today, in spite of the cold, I felt a strange exhilaration. In endless circles and flying as swiftly as the motor would carry me, I rose to a height of 8,500 feet in from twenty to twenty-five minutes. It was speedier than I had ever risen before and I had all I could do to attend to the machine.

A glance at the barograph strapped to my wrist told me I was in striking distance of the world's record. But suddenly my heart sank as I noticed that the little pencil on the barograph had ceased its upward tracing and was holding at an unsteady level. With victory in my very grasp, I could feel it slipping away from me.

Now I tried a trick which is considered risky 100 feet from the ground, but which most people experienced in the art of air flying would consider suicidal at such a height and in such thin atmosphere. Nursing my motor and almost rising from my seat in my eagerness, I pointed her nose directly upward . . . the little light roadster shivered and quivered, and slowly, very slowly, dug up into the air. Then followed the most nerve-racking battle of my life. It took me one hour to push her up from 8,500 feet to 9,700 feet. How I did it at the angle luck only knows. I was seated like a cowboy mounted on a bronco. My feet were jacked up and my head was lying back, as though reclining in a steep Morris chair.

Now and then the Morris chair and its stability would disappear, and I seemed to be reclining in a huge rocking chair. Half the time I was lying almost flat on my back and straining for a view of the angles.

It was thus, nursing the last remnants of power in the motor, and coaxing away my own fears, that I traveled up to 9,700 feet. I kept on going until my motor began to skip and stop. Then, saving the last drops of gasoline for the landing, I shut off the power and dropped earthward. The earth never seemed to rush up to meet me so speedily as now. It seemed as though Mother Earth was stretching out her hand to me.

The first aviation death in Europe came early in 1910, and soon that year there were twenty more. The first American pilot to die was Ralph Johnstone. Flying in a show in Denver on

November 17, he fell out of a spiral dive maneuver, the plane roaring almost straight down. The crash was close to the grandstand. Arch Hoxsey and Walter Brookins struggled to get Johnstone's body away from the grasp of souvenir seekers. The band continued to play.

On December 31 in Los Angeles, Arch Hoxsey was killed, his plane flipping over near the ground. Again, a crowd rushed forward.

In November of the following year, 1911, the Wrights closed down their exhibition business. They had lost Johnstone and Hoxsey. In 1912, two other pilots from the original team died in air show flying, another in a test flight for the army. A sixth man was killed in a flying accident in 1928.

Air show promoter Ross Browne recalled reading the papers during those years. "Every morning I would pick up the *Times* or the *Tribune* and with trepidation we'd look at it, expecting somebody to be killed. One would be killed in Chicago, or Erie, Pennsylvania. Hardly a week would go by that one of the boys whom we knew wasn't killed. Fellow that you'd been with, had eaten with. However, that was the early days of aviation and you had to take it as it came."

Browne started out as a pilot; he was trained in France by Roland Garros, and knew Wilbur Wright from the flights at Le Mans and Pau. He was interested in the show-business side of aviation, and helped organize the meet at Belmont Park. As that event got started, Browne noticed that no one could hear the announcements. So he hired Harry Lebrecque: "He had a voice like a foghorn, and he used two big megaphones, enormous megaphones. You could hear him in any part of the track and the grandstands, every word, who was flying—it was a marvelous thing. Incidentally, this Harry Lebrecque had made quite a name for himself, showing in Macy's window, Gimbel's, and Wanamakers. . . . He used to stand and never close his eyes or move and people used to think it was a dummy. It was quite an advertising thing at the time. He told me that he used to use belladonna in his eyes to keep his eyes from flickering. He said the longest he stayed was an hour and a half, and they had a dummy on the other side standing there. And once in a while they had the dummy fixed so that the dummy would move its hands and people would bet, 'That other one's the dummy.' He was quite a character."

After Belmont, Browne helped John Moisant and his brother Alfred put together a traveling air show, with French and American flyers, heading south to Virginia, Tennessee, Louisiana, Texas, and Mexico. They carried everything in train cars, including a big oval tent with an old Barnum and Bailey hand to oversee the roustabouts. Their advance man was from the circus as well, and Harry Lebrecque went along to do the announcing. This was the first "Flying Circus" tour, although that term would be used more famously during World War I to describe the vans and wagons and bright red airplanes of Baron von Richthofen's Fokker triplane squadron.

The Moisant troupe included Roland Garros, who would later fly for France and fame against the German aces. Garros said, "We were veritable Bohemians, and we were no different from high-wire walkers or weight lifters." Although they lost John Moisant in a crash outside New Orleans, it was mostly a carefree adventure, taking them even as far as Cuba.

One innovation has become an air show standard. Browne first tried it out during a show in Richmond:

"After each aviator came down and landed in the infield, we put him in an old Stearns car we had, touring car with the back down. We'd seat the aviator on the back seat and go down the stretch in front of the grandstand with the announcer announcing who it was, and what he was flying." At the Oshkosh air show you'll get a ground-level view of the flyers, thanks to Ross Browne: "LADIES AND GENTLEMEN, HOW ABOUT A BIG HAND FOR THREE-TIME AEROBATIC NATIONAL CHAMPION PATTY WAGSTAFF!"

There is a raucous nature to the afternoons at Oshkosh— pulsating music and wound-up announcers on the PA, the reverberant, twisting cascade of engine noise—but as I start to walk away I hear Mozart, a piano concerto. I look and find nothing in the sky until I notice everyone else is looking higher. And *there* is a white sailplane—a glider—starting the most gradual of descents, smoke ghosting from each wingtip.

Manfred Radius is the sailplane pilot. During the previous performer's act, he was being towed, in wide spirals, to 5,000 feet. A pause there, floating across the top of the aerial stage, then the release, the music starts, the smoke is on.

I had no idea what a sailplane could do. This one falls and spins like a leaf, dipping its long wings, then wafting up, turning over, tumbling. The craft seems weightless, at the wind's behest. It falls, nose first, gathering speed, then rises and rises and inverts, passing upside down through the top of the arc. Again a steep fall, a curving climb, and the wingtip smoke stands in the air—as a figure-eight. And when the sailplane rises against the substance of the air, its wings reaching, I notice a sensation of flight in my body, and I pull my arms back and bring my chest forward, waiting for the wind's rush.

Below, the crowd is quiet, watching the plane, which appears to be moving with the tempo and mood of the music. And I realize that—if time traveling would someday work—this is the moment I would like Wilbur and Orville to see.

I think of Orville almost motionless in the wind sweeping up Kill Devil Hills, and the beginning moments of Wilbur's first flight in France, the quick lift and tight banking left turn. This simple flying machine in the air above Oshkosh, without engine, without propeller, carried inside a trailer behind a truck from air show to air show, this would be the flying they'd admire.

Put them in lawn chairs at the edge of the flight line. Get them a soft drink and a plate from the Flying Rotarians Brat Fry and Corn Roast—and just watch their faces.

CHAPTER NINE

HAWTHORN HILL

THERE IS AN EMPTY HOUSE IN DAYTON, OHIO, THAT IS FULL of stories. I wanted to see it, to help understand what happened to Orville and his father and his sister Katharine, after the years of success and world acclaim, after the flying was over.

The Wrights' new house at the corner of Harmon and Park Avenues was large enough to deserve a name. From Bishop Milton Wright's diary, April 28, 1914: "We moved from 7 Hawthorn Street, Dayton, Ohio, to Hawthorn Hill, Harmon Ave., Oakwood, Ohio. . . . We arrived in an auto-taxicab at 3:45 afternoon." Katharine later recalled, "Orv had gone to New York and we moved while he was gone to save him the fuss and muss. It was a beautiful day, warm and sunny, and the redbuds were in full bloom."

The house has four two-story-high columns at the entrance, and a spacious and shaded side porch. The color of the brick is coffee with a lot of milk, and under moonlight the house appears white. Perhaps the name was to honor the family's long-time home on the West Side, but the Oakwood building site was known for its hawthorn trees, among many other varieties. Orville had asked his high school botany teacher, William Werthner, to walk the grounds with him. The bishop reports they put names to thirty-five different trees, and later himself noted sycamore, ash, pignut, and maples.

Oakwood is a suburb to the south of Dayton, a winding drive or trolley car ride up from the valley. Orville and Wilbur bought a seventeen-acre parcel that offered a hilltop view of the town, and the fireworks on the Fourth of July. A Dayton architectural firm designed a Colonial-style home with fifteen rooms. The drawings were sent to Wilbur, who was in Europe on business. He wrote back: "I see that most of the rooms are smaller than in the original plans, and only the price has been enlarged. You are wasting entirely too much space on halls. I see plainly that I am going to be put into one of the south bedrooms so I pro-pose a new plan for them. In any event I am going to have a bathroom of my own, so please make me one." Wilbur's insis-tence was noted, but he died two years before Hawthorn Hill was finished. An entry, later, in his father's diary said, "Oh, why did he go so soon?"

Bishop Wright became fond of long walks around the new neighborhood of Oakwood. He followed a half-mile circuit, sometimes extending it to a mile. Often he'd ask to be driven to Woodland Cemetery, to visit Wilbur's grave, and that of his wife, Susan. At home he took naps and read the *Encyclopaedia Britannica*. Milton Wright retired from the United Brethren

Church in 1905, but he kept up with the issues, writing an occasional article. He also worked on his family's genealogy—a lifetime devotion.

The bishop enjoyed the people he met around the dinner table at Hawthorn Hill: aviators, explorers, inventors, company presidents. At age eighty-five, he joined a women's suffrage march that Katharine had helped plan: "There were 44 college women, in the procession. Orville marched by my side. The sidewalks were lined by many thousands of respectful spectators."

His last diary entries are from the early months of 1917. "Orville and Katharine took supper down town. . . . The trees are covered with sleet all forenoon. . . . Scipio came. He weighs 16 pounds. He is a St. Bernard dog. He is a good-looking puppy. Katharine goes to-morrow to Oberlin to meet a committee on the meeting of her class of Alumni."

Milton Wright, age eighty-eight, died in his sleep before sunrise, April 3, 1917.

On a warm and breezy morning I had a chance to walk through the rooms and hallways of Hawthorn Hill. The caretaker, Rose Gray, had the front door and many of the windows open for the air. The house has a gracious foyer, high ceilings, Oriental rugs on polished floors; woodwork that originally was dark-stained is now painted white. In the basement there's a workshop and a walk-in safe. A vast, echoing attic has a pull-down staircase that leads to the roof and a widow's walk, enclosed by a white balustrade.

Rose showed me through the dining room, the kitchen, the parlor, and Orville's study. "This is the only room that's been left as it was. Those are all his books. There's even his favorite old chair." It's a worn and stained brown fabric wingback with a substantial footstool. A side table holds a lamp and his reading glasses. Photographs of Orville's mother and father and Katharine are among the framed pictures on top of the oak bookcases. This room was originally the library, and Orville and Katharine would often work here together.

Katharine left to be married in the fall of 1926. Her brother lived alone for the next twenty-two years, with the help of Carrie Grumbach, the family's cook and housekeeper. Katharine was to return only in death. It is her story that I think of when I visit Hawthorn Hill, and when I return again and again to the photographs of the lovely home.

Katharine's letters from this period have been saved in the archives of the Western Historical Manuscript Collection in Kansas City. My entry into her world is by way of a microfilm reader at a library near my home. Photocopied handwritten pages float across the glass screen from right to left, the script black against a white background. I can examine a single sentence or watch the months and the years evolve in ethereal motion.

Katharine was only fifteen years old when her mother died. Prep school and college lay ahead, and a teaching career, but she knew of her father's expectations. He wrote to her even before Susan Wright's death: "Take especially good care of yourself. You have a good mind and good heart, and being my only daughter, you are my hope of love and care, if I live to be old."

The bishop, in his journals, had remarked on a couple of young men who came calling on Katharine and stayed for dinner. And once she had even been engaged, according to a letter she wrote to a friend, years later. But Katharine entered middle age unmarried, uncomplaining. After Wilbur's death and the bishop's passing, her brother Orville, three years older than she, became the absolute center of her life. It was that closeness that was to be the despair of both.

The man Katharine married in 1926, when she was fifty-two and he was fifty-four, was Henry J. Haskell, known to his friends as Harry. He was a widower; both Katharine and Orville had known and liked Isabel, his wife. Harry and Katharine had met at Oberlin College, near Cleveland. His class was '96, hers '98. For a time they lived in the same off-campus rooming house. Haskell was born in Ohio to a missionary family—as a teenager he spent three years in Bulgaria. He wanted to be a writer; after Oberlin, he sold two short stories and then gave up fiction for newspaper work. By 1910 he was married, had a son, and was directing the editorial page of the *Kansas City Star*. Katharine and Harry would see each other on visits to Oberlin, for homecoming and alumni meetings, and kept up a friendly correspondence between Dayton and Kansas City throughout the years after college.

In May of 1922, when Harry's wife was ill with cancer, Katharine wrote to offer sympathy, and also to express her admiration for his devotion to Isabel: "Sometimes I think of when we were in college and of how you have become the kind of man I thought you would. I always thought you would be like a rock when it came to strength and dependability and you have been just that."

The following year, in a long note about politics and literature, Katharine reassured Harry about his career in Kansas City:

"I have always smiled over your admiration of the men you see down East, imagining that you are 'crude' in comparison! That's really funny and Orv thinks so, too. What a blessed relief it is, though, to find one modest person, among writers!"

Isabel Haskell died in September 1923. As that winter began, Harry took his son on a European trip, and wrote to Katharine from various spots along the way. She told Harry, in reply, that his travel notes made her happy: "It recalls my first experience in Europe and I can see that it strikes you much as it did me. Your joy at the Stoke Poges church struck a responsive chord. Wasn't that old yew tree the loveliest old thing? 'Beneath that sacred elm, that yew tree's shade.'" In this letter Katharine added a note about Orville, who was having trouble with pain in his leg, but, she said, "When he gets back to his usual condition, SOMETHING is going to happen about the book."

Orville suffered from sciatica, caused by his injuries in the 1908 Fort Myer crash, and it often sent him to bed for days at a time, providing a reason not to be working on an account of the early flying experiments. If his brother had lived, they would have finished the book together and it would be on every library shelf in America. Wilbur enjoyed writing and handled most of the scientific work for the lawsuits. Orville hated to write, but his technical articles and letters are superb.

Katharine offered to help. She would organize the material, and track down old references. Orville's secretary, at his laboratory on Dayton's West Side, could take dictation. A "Houghton Mifflin man" came to Hawthorn Hill to talk it over. But it was becoming clear that Orville could neither write the book nor abandon the idea.

✢ ✢

On December 26, 1923, Katharine told Harry she had "survived" both Christmas and the anniversary of the first flight, saying, "We are glad that the twentieth anniversary can only come once in a life-time."

The celebration on the seventeenth was organized by Dayton's National Cash Register Company, and included lunch at Hawthorn Hill. Katharine said all the kindness was appreciated, but her words have a touch of scorn: "The truth was murdered enough in that day to make you weep. The Cash Register was in its glory. The publicity department was in charge. You can imagine the rest. I had to take my little brother aside and tell him to play the game for he couldn't stand the idea of letting that press agent gang come around our house. General Patrick ordered one of every kind of plane at McCook and Wilbur Wright Fields to fly over our house in the afternoon. We all jumped up and left our luncheon for about ten minutes. It was a pretty sight."

By March 1924, Harry Haskell had returned to Kansas City from Europe and was back at his desk at the *Star*. He was still sad after Isabel's death, writing to Katharine about "dark and forbidding things" he found, coming home. She answered, "Tomorrow is your birthday and I hope this letter will get to you then. Orv and I thought of it and wished we could remember you in some happy way. I'll soon be fifty myself before long. I hope you have many, many happy years ahead of you. It is possible, I am sure."

And Katharine in turn asked Harry for advice in the spring of 1924, saying that she was "horribly dissatisfied to be doing nothing," and that "no one ought to be living without some work." Her brother's book project had been only an unlikely hope. She hadn't taught high school since 1908, when she went to

Washington, D.C., to help take care of Orville. Later she traveled with her brothers in Europe, then never returned to the classroom. She said, "I really like to teach but Orv won't listen to that and it is too taxing."

In November 1924, Katharine and Harry got into a discussion about widows, or "vidders," as he had put it, who seemed overly aggressive, and about the nature of women in general. She told him, "I don't agree with you that the men are more interesting, broader in their interests than the women. We sniff at Women's Clubs sometimes but was *any* Women's Club ever so silly as the Rotary and that whole string of clubs?"

Early in January 1925, Katharine wrote to thank Harry for a scarf he'd sent as a Christmas present. Her letters were usually quite long, and her appreciation of a scarf could lead to a description of a new velvet evening gown with its changeable tones, and her love and understanding of color and then her desire to know more about form. "Did I ever tell you about my first spectacles?" she wrote. "When I was eleven years old a cousin who was staying with us for some time discovered that I was near-sighted. She was so herself and recognized it in me. I got my glasses in November, I remember. I was wild with delight. But particularly the trees were so beautiful. They are so interesting, some so graceful, some with very lacy branches, as the ironwood. I never come in our entrance on a winter day that I don't notice the trees outlined against the sky on the west."

Later in January 1925, for the first time in the letters, she called Harry "dear," and it seems likely he had mentioned his desire to marry her. Their correspondence had become a courtship, with envelopes crossing the Midwest in the mail cars of fast trains. Often she mailed two letters a day; there are thousand of pages on the microfilm.

As 1925 began, Katharine Wright was fifty years old, deliriously in love and also desperately fearful of that notion. She hoped for courage to someday tell her brother that she wanted to marry and leave home, and for the time being she believed Orville had no idea what was going on.

She used simple stationery, with HAWTHORN HILL, OAKWOOD, DAYTON, OHIO centered in print at the top. The early letters to Harry had been typewritten, but after love was declared her voice turns to a whisper—she wrote most often in her bedroom, in a clear and tidy script.

On Saturday night, April 4, she wrote: "I just want you to know, Mister, that you can't write me a love letter, such as I got today, and send me flowers, such as I got today, without getting a love letter back! The letter was so dear and the flowers so lovely. Carrie arranged the flowers in the basket that came from you two years ago." And Katharine recalled a recent overnight visit Harry made to Hawthorn Hill, staying in what she referred to as the blue room. She hoped it could happen again: "And you know we really need the blue room. . . . It was such a sweet place to love you, with the lovely moonlight for our only light."

During these years Harry Haskell became caught up in Orville's plans to send the 1903 Flyer to the Science Museum in London, rather than the Smithsonian Institution. The Wrights, loyal to the Smithsonian, had offered to put the '03 aircraft back together and ship it to Washington, but the Smithsonian's reply lacked enthusiasm: "Inasmuch as the machine used at Fort Myer has attracted such world-wide interest, that machine, if it can be repaired or reconstructed, would seem most suitable. If, however, the Wright brothers think the Kitty Hawk machine would answer the purpose, their judgment might decide the question."

The brothers didn't trust Smithsonian Secretary Charles Walcott enough to follow up and see what "might" really meant. And they could envision their 1908 Fort Myer plane on display next to Samuel P. Langley's full-size 1903 machine, the Great Aerodrome. Never mind that it crashed into the Potomac River on takeoff; the message would be clear—but incorrect—that Langley's was first in the air.

In 1914 the Aerodrome *did* fly, after the Smithsonian allowed Glenn Curtiss to take the wrecked craft and its engine out of storage and see if he could make it airworthy. At his shop in Hammondsport, New York, Curtiss improved Langley's flawed wing design, changed the steering system, fixed up the engine, put the plane on floats, and flew it for 150 feet out over a lake.

Then the Aerodrome was rebuilt in reverse—returned to its 1903 form—and displayed in the Smithsonian's Arts and Industries building as "the first man-carrying aeroplane in the history of the world capable of sustained free flight."

Judging the Langley Aerodrome display card to be deliberately deceitful, Orville refused to show his plane at the Smithsonian. A compromise was offered, a change in the wording of the Langley display, but the term "capable of flight" remained. In 1916 Orville reassembled his 1903 Flyer and sent it to an exhibit in Boston, and later New York and Dayton. By then he had decided to accept an offer to display the plane at the Science Museum in London.

"No one could possibly regret more than I do that our

machine must go into a foreign museum," Orville wrote, responding to an inquiry. "It is not safe where it is. It suffered in one flood and has always been liable to fire." And he openly stated his purpose: "In a foreign museum this machine will be a constant reminder of the reasons for its being there, and after the people and petty jealousies of this day are gone, the historians of the future may examine the evidence impartially and make history accord with it. Your regret that this old machine must leave the country can hardly be so great as my own."

Katharine, too, was involved in the Smithsonian controversy. On May 11, 1925, she wrote to Harry on Orville's behalf: "He is sitting here and while I have the chance I am going to get him to tell me what to say." She went on for three pages, laying out Orville's position on several points of the argument. Then: "Orville deserted me long ago, just as I finished the first page. He is very tired. In fact I am worried about him. He was all right until last Friday when the *N.Y. World* man was here. He was here Thursday and Friday. Orv was frantic with that job of trying to explain anything to him when he didn't know what an aileron was."

On May 12 there was a professional exchange of telegrams:

[TO] ORVILLE WRIGHT. CARE OAKWOOD DAYTON OHIO. HAVE YOU MADE ANY STATEMENT ABOUT THE PLANS FOR LENGTH OF STAY OF PLANE IN LONDON WOULD YOU PLEASE WIRE US COLLECT BRIEF STATEMENT OF WHAT YOU WISH SAID ON SUBJECT. H.J. HASKELL

[TO] HARRY J. HASKELL. CARE OF THE KANSAS CITY STAR. PROBABLY PERMANENT BUT PREFER SAY NOTHING. ORVILLE WRIGHT

In an unsigned *Kansas City Star* editorial on May 18, Harry wrote: "By its placard on the rebuilt Langley machine the Smithsonian Institution has claimed for its former secretary something that he never claimed for himself—the priority in this revolutionary invention. Langley had failed to solve the theory of flight in three essential points . . . [which] had been solved independently by the brilliant researches of the Wright brothers. The proof lay in the successful flight of their plane following the collapse of the Langley machine."

Katharine's letter had clearly been a briefing for Harry's editorial. Orville sent a gift to Kansas City, in thanks. Harry wrote back, "Dear Orv: I couldn't have had anything that would please me so much as the photograph of the first flight that came this morning. How fortunate it was that the photographer was so successful."

Almost all of Katharine's letters display moments of hopeful exuberance, tempered by paragraphs of doubt. On January 11, 1925, she wrote, "It scares me to have you love me so much. I love it but it scares me. It makes me want to beg you not to think so much of me—for fear of—well, for fear of things that do happen sometimes. I'm not young, dear, for one thing. But, dear, you couldn't stand another hard time."

When she realized that Harry was serious about marriage, Katharine tried to explain what she saw as the difference between love and simple affection: "I hadn't considered 'loving you' and you really gave me a great shock by telling me that you loved me and had loved me from those far off days in Oberlin. . . . There were two reasons why I fancied I could be as good friends as I wanted to be with men. One reason was that

I had Orv who was more like a lover than a brother (in some ways!)—someone else said that of him. And the other was that my experiences and observations were that these men were not inclined to have 'feelings' about me."

June 16, 1925: "You spoke, in the letter that came today, about my having the same right to satisfy my own heart that Orv would have had and that everybody would have thought it was all right if he had married without considering me. But, dear, Orv *didn't* want to leave me." Katharine added in another letter: "Will and Orv have made my life—most of my interests, since Oberlin days and before. There was a reason why none of us married. I am sure Will and Orv thought as much of me as of themselves when they made any plans. We all planned this house together. Orv and I made changes on the second floor because Will was gone when we actually began to build. And Orv loves his home so, too. Of course, he likes the way I keep house. We grew up with the same ideas."

In July of 1925 Katharine and Orville began making plans for their annual stay in Canada, on Lake Huron. Orville had bought a summer compound, with several buildings and a boat dock, on Lambert Island, in Georgian Bay. They invited Harry to take some vacation time and join them. Before the trip, Katharine wrote: "I am as discouraged about the Smithsonian business as I have ever been. So I am beginning to think that all this depression and hopelessness is mostly very tired nerves. Orv looks awfully thin and is much more quiet than usual . . . and the best way to get something done next fall is not to let Orv worry or think about that stuff any more than he can help. He is like a boy at the Bay. You can hear him singing anytime almost. . . .

Here is a little picture I took of a corner of our island. The houses are perched away up on the rock—uglier than sin, the houses are, but comfortable, and the rock and water are *lovely.*"

After Harry's visit, Katharine wrote often from Georgian Bay, once while "boldly" sitting at the table where Orville was playing solitaire: "Your visit was so lovely, dear, not only for us, of course it was lovely for us, but Orv enjoyed it too. He was so glad to see you looking better all the time, he said. He thought you were very nervous and 'jumpy' when you came. (I did not notice that so distinctly.) He said he thought you began to take on a 'rested' look."

Another surreptitiously written letter—on October 7—came to Harry on stationery from the Hotel Pennsylvania. Katharine and Orville were in New York City for the air races, and Orville had two aviation banquets to attend. They bought some china at Tiffany's, they saw a play together. In the evening, while her brother was downstairs dining on filet of sole Florentine with potatoes Duchesse, and listening to a speech by Captain Eddie Rickenbacker, Katharine was at the writing table in their sitting room, dreaming about being married and living in Kansas City: "After we tell everybody what's going to happen, I can come to K.C. and we can see what I need to get ready and so on. I like to talk about it, too, for it makes me feel as if I were really going to be with you and have our home together."

Katharine outlined her financial standing for Harry, saying she wanted to bring along the silver from Hawthorn Hill; it was a service that Wilbur and Orville had started for her the Christmas after the first flight. She had $30,000 in Liberty Bonds, part ownership of land in Cleveland, the house on Hawthorn Street, which the bishop had deeded to her, a one-fourth share in a farm in Indiana, and an extra thousand dollars she had saved. She wrote, "I'm glad I've got a little to bring with me, dear." And she daydreamed about Harry's house in Kansas City. They would have a study with a "rich Oriental rug and one big chair for two! Simple things will be lovely in the bedrooms. You keep your eyes open for twin beds."

She longed for a normal, everyday sort of life. Once she told Harry about going to a nice place for dinner with Orville: "I couldn't keep from thinking how it would be to go out with you that way. You see we've never even once been out to dinner alone. Oh, Harry—wouldn't we see Europe together? And wouldn't we troop around everywhere, hand-in-hand, and have the gayest time?"

In May of 1926, after more than a year of anxiety and indecision, Katharine told Orville that she was in love. Harry made a brief stop on his way to Washington, D.C., and spoke with Orville as well. Two days later Katharine wrote to Harry, "I wonder if we could be married pretty soon. I'll do what I said I would, dear. I won't back out now." In this letter her pen strokes were firm, and dark with ink. She struggled to stay in control through her writing: "I feel just as if someone in the family had died. This is the first time there has been any trouble to amount to anything between Orville and me. He looks so pitiful, so dark under his eyes—just as he used to look when he was terribly worried and sick besides. . . . You know, dear, you said the other night that it was pretty late for me to speak of being uneasy about what we were doing. That went in deep with me. It was so true and there was no way out."

She put her pen down after that statement, but continued the next day: "Orv won't stay in the house a minute. He went away before half past six this morning. I *can't* stand it, dear. I am so sick I can hardly keep going but I must. I do love you. A sweet kiss." Harry's quick reply seems sympathetic but not very helpful: "Your letter has just arrived. I understand perfectly. But K dear, dear K, I care for you too much to let you go ahead against your better judgment and just because you said you would. . . . There wouldn't be happiness for either of us in that. No dear, the only possible thing to do is to face the facts and act on them. Only dear, we want to be very sure we know what the facts are. I couldn't possibly ask you to do what you thought you shouldn't."

Katharine's next letter was mailed two days later, May 16: "Dearest, I didn't know what to do so I told Orv not to worry. I wasn't going to leave him now. He didn't sleep a wink for two nights and was taking aspirin. I had to comfort him last night. He said last night he couldn't say a word, he was so sick. I'm glad it is all right out-and-out, dear. I do love you so."

Harry visited Hawthorn Hill again to speak with Orville, making it clear that Katharine would leave, but not right away. Vacation time came, and Orville and Katharine went as usual to Lambert Island, avoiding any talk of her marriage. September came and Katharine found she still couldn't talk with Orville. She wrote to Harry and said, "I have started four times but I can't get anywhere when I see that look on his face." And she wanted Harry's assurance that she'd still be able to look after Orville if she married: "You *will* let me keep right on with my care of him, won't you dear?"

Finally, on November 13, Katharine told Harry about her decision to have a small out-of-town wedding at the home of friends. She had asked her older brother Lorin and his wife to help. "I have just sent you a telegram, dear. Lorin talked to Orv today and we find that he will not be at the wedding and will not allow me to use his name on our announcements. So we can't have any announcements and we think it would be better to have the wedding at Oberlin. We are trying to arrange so no one will know that Orv is not there."

A newspaper account stated: "On November 20th Miss Katharine Wright, sister of the Wright Brothers, inventors of the airplane, was married at Oberlin, Ohio, to Mr. Henry Joseph Haskell, chief editorial writer and associate editor of the *Kansas City Star.* The ceremony was performed by Dr. Henry Churchill King, president of Oberlin College, where both bride and groom attended." Lorin and Netta Wright were not present, only their daughter Leontine Jameson and her husband, John, who lived in nearby Cleveland.

At least two newspapers reported, incorrectly, that Orville Wright was in attendance at the wedding. In Kansas City, the *Star*'s story concluded, "Mr. and Mrs. Haskell will be at home after January 1 at 4500 Charlotte Street."

Orville's thoughts during these difficult years have not been shared. Most of Harry's letters to Katharine have apparently been destroyed. The story can only be told from the perspective of her correspondence, from the archival collection donated by the Haskell family. But the real tragedy, for me, arises simply from the facts of record. A brother and sister find themselves wrenched apart by circumstance and anger and passion and stubborn pride. Given time, there would be hope of reconciliation. With Katharine's death, that opportunity was too quickly lost.

After the wedding and the move to Kansas City, Katharine and her brother remained apart. A letter that she sent to Orville in

Dayton was returned unopened. The final item in the Katharine Wright Haskell collection is dated March 11, 1927, four months after her marriage. It was a reply to her friend Agnes Beck, who had written from Dayton to ask how Katharine was doing.

Your letter made me homesick—almost the first time I have felt really homesick. It is a rainy day, too, and I haven't been out of the house. I may stir out after a while and go down on the [trolley] car to drive out home with Harry. We are going to dinner tonight at Mrs. Hill's. Dr. Hill was President of the University of Missouri but resigned not very long after marrying a very rich woman. I have never got dinner but once since I have been here. And we have never gone out to a restaurant yet—or one of Harry's clubs. . . . I go to Oberlin again in three weeks for a trustees' meeting. I'll not stay longer than my business keeps me, since I can't go home I want to get out of Ohio as soon as I can. Many thanks for the invitation to visit you. I would love to do it but I can't go to Dayton yet. Lorin thinks I ought to come to see them but I can't do it yet. In my imagination I walk through the house, looking for Little Brother, and at all the dear familiar things that made my home. But I never find Little Brother and I have lost my old home forever, I fear. Harry is so unbelievably good to me and is so happy about my being here that I can't spoil his happiness. Carrie writes to me often and says she has suggested several times that he ask some friends in to dinner but he "just smiles," she says. I am sure she is taking good care of O.W. I must take a Dayton paper. I have intended to subscribe but keep forgetting to do

so. Please write when you can. I haven't had many letters. I suppose pretty much every body was offended.

In March of 1929, after two years and three months of marriage,
Katharine Wright Haskell died of pneumonia, at home in
Kansas City. She was fifty-four years old. After the funeral Harry
wrote to one of their friends in London, describing her illness—
severe chills, a temperature of 104. He said he had called Lorin
in Dayton and asked that Orville also be told that Katharine was
dangerously ill: "On Saturday morning when Lorin came we
were able to arouse her for a moment. When Orville arrived she
was still weaker. I asked her if she knew him, and finally she
aroused and said 'of course I do.' But that was all. She was
unconscious until her death Sunday evening. We had the
Episcopalian service at the house Monday and left for Dayton
that night. Services were at Orville's Wednesday and she was
buried beside Wilbur. . . . I felt she had been so long identified
with Dayton she would have liked to be buried there. . . .
I believe she had two interesting and happy years in Kansas City.
They were wonderful years for me."

At the time of her illness Katharine had been getting her
clothes together for a trip with Harry to Italy and Greece; they'd
booked passage on the *Roma,* sailing for Naples. Later, Harry
donated money to Oberlin College for a small marble foun-
tain—the design inspired by one he had seen in Florence—to
be built in Katharine's honor, outside the art museum.

Harry Haskell remarried and, in 1946, became a widower for
the third time. He won two Pulitzer Prizes, one for his editori-
als and one for the entire editorial page. He died in 1952, at
seventy-eight. Harry and Orville had maintained a cordial rela-
tionship. In the Library of Congress you can find two faded

telegrams from May 1929, just two months after Katharine's death:

[TO] ORVILLE WRIGHT = HARMON AND PARK AVES
DAYTON OHIO=

WILL SPEND SATURDAY IN DAYTON ARRIVING SATURDAY
MORNING. H.J. HASKELL

[TO] HENRY J. HASKELL C/O K.C. STAR

WILL BE LOOKING FOR YOU IN THE PENN AMERICAN
TOMORROW MORNING. ORVILLE WRIGHT

At Hawthorn Hill the Wright family bedrooms are all on the second floor: Orville's, the bishop's, the room that would have been Wilbur's, and Katharine's. Hers has tall, lace-curtained, glass-paned doors that open onto a narrow balcony. When I was there I asked Rose Gray, "Is that where Lindbergh stood? Can I go out?" "Surely," she laughed, opening the doors.

In 1927 a suddenly famous Charles Lindbergh stepped onto this balcony and grinned and waved to a crowd that had spilled across the driveway below and out over the lawn. He'd come to Hawthorn Hill for an overnight stay on his way home, flying his small plane, the *Spirit of St. Louis,* to Dayton. A photo shows Lindbergh wearing a leather flying cap, and Orville a straw boater, together in the back of an open car. Orville seems thrilled. He was in the company of a fellow pilot—twenty-five years old—

who had flown nonstop from New York to Paris in thirty-three hours, winning a $25,000 prize.

Had Katharine not married and left, she would have been the one to plan that evening's dinner for Charles Lindbergh, and would have delighted at hearing the young aviator's stories.

In 1948, when he was seventy-seven, Orville Wright died after a heart attack. He had never married, and had lived quietly at Hawthorn Hill, driving himself to his West Side laboratory each day in a current-year Hudson with the license plate "OW-1." Orville often took lunch and sometimes dinner at the Engineers Club of Dayton; he'd helped found the club and was one of its first presidents. His family remained close, especially Lorin's children and grandchildren, and "Uncle Orv" took great pleasure in hosting Thanksgiving and Christmas dinners at Hawthorn Hill. He gave a few interviews, traveled for consulting work and to accept awards, but never made a speech longer than "Thank you." At night he was known to walk through the Oakwood neighborhood, and if he saw a light on at a friend's house he'd knock on the door. "Well, it's just Orville," he'd say. "I just wondered if you cared for company."

CHAPTER TEN

FIRST FLIGHT

IN A TWENTY-MILE-AN-HOUR WIND, AN AVIATOR'S WHITE SILK scarf, held aloft at ground level, will almost fly itself—becoming a lustrous horizontal stream.

I've come to Kill Devil Hills on December 17, in early morning. Sunlight glances onto the sandy plain of the Wright Brothers National Memorial site. The wind is from the northeast. Those who travel every year to the Outer Banks for this day always hope for clear skies and to see the wind strong off the ocean. And they wait for the anniversary moment of the Wright brothers' first powered flight, at 10:35 A.M.

The scarf I've brought is for warmth as well as for style. And I have a handheld anemometer so I can check the wind speeds. Three small black plastic cups spin and a needle rises across red markings on a white scale. Mostly it's twenty miles per hour, with dips to fifteen and gusts to twenty-five. In 1903 the Wrights worked through the morning in this chilly wind—

a force that stiffens your body, dries your eyes, makes you duck your head and turn away.

Some people, older couples, wait in their strategically parked vehicles, motors running. For them it's a drive-in air show. They'll see ninety-nine aircraft appear in the sky to their left, the southwest, then bank in for a low pass over the crowd.

Everyone else is out in jeans and coveralls and parkas and even mink coats. They have provisions of hot coffee and egg sandwiches, and carry fleece-bundled babies, camp chairs, binoculars and cameras. Official welcomes and tributes are being offered from a platform in front of the visitors' center, but most everyone's come for the airplanes, and the distinguished words escape the PA speakers and dance off in the wind.

The band stops playing. An announcer stands ready. He's watching the "air boss"—an air force officer who's coordinating the incoming flights. Planes from all over the United States are converging on this tiny point on the map of the North Carolina coast. They come from home bases in Texas, New York, Missouri, New Mexico, Louisiana—to arrive on schedule and sweep down through a vector over the monument grounds. The air boss speaks into a handheld UHF radio; he's talking to the pilots and navigators, and a controller on nearby Roanoke Island. He looks to the southwest and nods to the announcer: the first aircraft is on approach.

Ninety-nine years ago on this morning, Wilbur Wright, I'd guess, had his pocket watch out to note the time when his brother released their airplane on its takeoff roll along the sixty-foot wooden track: the flight was over at 10:35:12. If I were flying lead-off for today's ninety-nine-aircraft Kill Devil Hills flyby—if I were the pilot of the air force B-2 Spirit stealth bomber—I'd want to try to get down low over the crowd within that twelve-second time span. Aviation people—the newspapers call them "propellerheads"—are serious enough to notice.

If, in a time warp, Wilbur Wright would look up and see the stealth bomber approaching, he wouldn't recognize it as an airplane. It seems more like an immense black boomerang that a strange force has flung through the sky. It's a V-shaped wing with a jagged rear edge. It carries conventional or nuclear payloads. Stealth technology hides it from radar.

The plane slides in through the thin clouds to the west, turns north, and is suddenly past—overhead. Thunderous low-frequency sound stays behind in the air. The announcer says, "Ladies and gentlemen, from Whiteman Air Force Base in Missouri, the B-2 Stealth bomber."

These are training missions for the air force, navy, and marines. Get the planes up and working, and why not run down to North Carolina for a tightly coordinated flyby? And it's handy to have the monument as a landmark. Sixty feet high, built on top of a ninety-foot coastal sand dune, the monument has an aeronautical design, resembling a pylon of the kind formerly used at turning points in air races. It's an immense triangle of North Carolina granite blocks with the word FAITH at the north-facing apex.

Several civilian planes are in the lineup, including a local favorite. Scott Challice of Kitty Hawk Aero Tours comes puttering overhead in a glossy blue-and-yellow Waco biplane. Built in 1941 as a navy trainer, with open twin cockpits, the Waco has a visual kinship with the Wright Flyer. I've been up with Scott, lifting off from the small airport on Roanoke Island. I climbed into the front seat. He handed me some goggles and said, "Watch those pedals, they're hot." Then, "Contact," as he started the engine. We crossed the waters of Albemarle Sound

to fly over Jockey's Ridge and then circled the Wright
Monument, with the plane banked steeply so I could see better.
I reminded myself to relax and let my body accept the angle. On
east over the surf line, and Scott tapped my shoulder and yelled,
"See the dolphins playing?" When the water's clearer, he told
me, you can see shipwreck remains on the ocean floor.

On this morning the Waco makes its slow pass and turns for
home. Then an air force refueling tanker plane drifts by, with a
boom extended from its tail. The announcer spots an incoming
formation of jet fighters, "If you liked the motion picture *Top
Gun,* here's the plane the famous Mr. Tom Cruise pretended to
fly: the F-14 supersonic Tomcat, built by Grumman." Next,
"the real heroes of the Gulf War: the A-10 Warthog close support attack fighter." An Avenger flies over, followed by the Wild
Weasels. We see the Talon, the Jayhawk, the Nighthawk,
Hornet, and Falcon. And over a shriek of engines the
announcer says, "Ladies and gentlemen, the Navy Strike
Eagles—the sound of freedom!"

The last plane crosses overhead. The good-byes and thank-yous
are announced, the dignitaries leave, the TV crews retreat, the
crowd wanders off. And in the wind, in the silence, I hear the
Quaker hymn "Simple Gifts." The Northeastern High School
Orchestral Band struggles with the notes in the cold.
Northeastern is in Elizabeth City, where Wilbur first arrived by
train in 1900, looking for a way across Albemarle Sound, now
about an hour away by road. The town's been proud of its
Wright heritage, and the Northeastern band has provided music
for decades' worth of December 17 celebrations. I've seen pic-

tures from the early years; they would play as they marched, in a winding line, up the hill to the monument.

The Northeastern band sits on metal chairs on the grass, performing, at this moment, mostly just for their director, Wayne James, and perhaps a few parents. The uniforms are dark green and gold; some members wear earmuffs, no one has a hat. Mr. James calls for "Stars and Stripes," and I can hear him talking in a kind and quiet voice to his youngsters as they try to sort out their sheet music. "I know you're complaining, I'm not saying it's not cold out here, but there are people who are colder than you are and don't know where their next meal is coming from."

He straightens and gives the downbeat for the march that John Philip Sousa wrote in 1896 and that the Wrights surely heard played in their honor. As "The Stars and Stripes Forever" nears the last chorus, there's a slowing of tempo. It's where the emotional tug begins. The piccolo player stands, along with the cornets and trombones, and the song soars to its timpani-and-cymbal finale. A laughing Wayne James thanks his band.

This day of honor, December 17, was, in 1903, the end of an often-arduous flying season that began late in September.

From Orville's diary: "Reached Norfolk at 11:30, and Elizabeth City at 5:30 p.m. where we took the *Ocracoke* to Roanoke Island. We reached Manteo at 1:30 a.m. Friday."

Then Orville wrote his sister Katharine from Kill Devil Hills: "We reached camp Friday noon, having come over from Manteo in a small gasoline launch. The building, however, is several feet nearer the ocean than when we left last year. . . . We were glad to find, on reaching camp, that our groceries and tools had not been burned in the depot fire at Elizabeth City, and that the lumber was here ready for building. I put in most of my time Friday afternoon and yesterday morning making a 'French drip' coffeepot.

"Have Lorin mount four or five of those pictures of the Life Saving Station. Also have him get a piece of the very finest mesh brass-wire screen, about 4″ × 8″. He can get it at some of the tinners over in town. We want it for our coffeepot. . . ."

Orville closes with, "Good-bye." And adds a postscript: "Have the wire screen sent on immediately."

On file back in Dayton were pictures the Wrights had taken at the Kitty Hawk Life-Saving Station. Orville wanted prints to give to the crew members. By the 1890s, snapshots were popular. In 1900 you could buy a Kodak Brownie camera for one dollar and a film cartridge for twenty-five cents. But the Wrights used larger-format cameras, with higher resolution. They intended to carefully document a scientific process, but probably could not imagine their pictures would someday be used in their intense legal battles to enforce their patents.

In the summer of 1902 they replaced their four-by-five-inch negative camera with a Korona V, ordered from Rochester, New York, at a cost of $55.55. The Korona, a wooden view camera, used five-by-seven-inch glass photographic plates. It came with a variable-distance lens, a tripod, and a black focusing cloth. Including a supply of plates in canvas cases, it would be quite an outfit to transport—by buggy, train, boat, and pony cart—to the camp on the Outer Banks, then back to Dayton.

Each of the four years the brothers came to the beach, they brought a new plane. In 1903 they also brought a motor and propellers. They built a new shed to house the '03 Flyer and started putting it together, stretching the cloth, rigging the wires, and occasionally taking time out to fly the previous year's glider, which had been left in its original hangar. October went by, then November; they took photographs as the Flyer took shape. The engine was causing trouble, running rough, damaging the two propeller shafts, which had to be sent to a real machine shop—their own in Dayton. One of the shafts that Charlie Taylor repaired and shipped back cracked, and so Orville took the train to Dayton to have new ones made from stronger steel.

December's cold came, with ice on the rainwater ponds and high winds pushing the stinging sand. In earlier years, with the weather sure to turn worse, they'd been home by now. This year they intended to be home for Christmas, having flown or not.

On the thirteenth the plane was ready. The wind, though, was down. On the morning of the fourteenth they decided to try a takeoff with a slight downhill run. The surfmen from the Kill Devil Hills station came to help move the plane to a low slope of the dune that the Wrights called Big Hill. The wooden sections of the launching rail were laid out. A picture was taken, showing four men, two small boys, and a dog gathered near the left wingtip. The propellers were spun, starting up the motor. The boys, it is said, ran off, scared by the noise. Wilbur won a coin toss, lay at the center of the bottom wing, and started down the rail. A fine photograph shows the craft on the sand, the bottom of the front elevator buried, Wilbur with his left hand on the control stick and a jut to his jaw. He'd risen some fifteen feet, too steep, too fast—and stalled. They decided not to count it as a flight.

Repair work on the fifteenth, no wind on the sixteenth, then success on the seventeenth. Five men were there to help and witness and tell the stories afterward. And pictures were taken for the same purpose.

Orville carried the Korona and its wooden tripod out to the right side of the intended flight path. He bent under the black cloth and brought the launching rail into bright focus—upside down—on the ground glass. The composition was a guess. If the machine was to lift off, it might happen *there,* forty feet down the track. He asked lifesaver Daniels to take the picture *if* the plane rose: Just stand right here and hold on to this rubber bulb and click the shutter when you see daylight under the plane. Orville slid in a film holder, pulled out the dark slide so the camera was ready. Then he got set to fly.

John T. Daniels of the U.S. Life-Saving Service, and Manteo, North Carolina, is the photographer of record for the first flight of a powered aircraft. He would always maintain it was the only picture he took in his life. But at 10:36 that morning no one was sure that Daniels *had* squeezed the bulb and opened the shutter. The glass negative would be labeled and packed away, for developing in Dayton.

The second flight, with Wilbur as the pilot, was also very short and was not photographed. A poorly focused but dramatic photo exists from flight number three, showing Orville banking to the right as he kept the plane up for a few seconds longer. Then it was Wilbur's turn again, and the photograph of his flight shows the plane still in the air and quite far from the camera. Almost a minute of flying time, and a distance of 852 feet.

The brothers and the volunteers carried the five-hundred-sixty-pound Flyer back to the launching rail, the gusting northeast wind against the wings providing a helpful lift. They took another picture of the plane, this time at rest, with Big Hill rising in the background. They talked about trying a flight up the beach to the weather station at Kitty Hawk—four miles away. But in a sudden jumble of twisting wire and shattering wood, the machine was wrecked, flipped over by the wind. John Daniels tried to hold a rising wing and got caught up with the chains and engine. It was an awful sight, but he was unhurt.

Talking with a reporter many years later, Daniels recalled his experience that day. In his mind, over time, it had become a colorful fantasy.

"I like to think about it now; I like to think about that first airplane the way it sailed off in the air at Kill Devil Hills. . . . I don't think I ever saw a prettier sight in my life. Its wings and uprights were braced with new and shiny copper piano wires. The sun was shining bright that morning, and the wires just blazed in the sunlight like gold. The machine looked like some big, graceful golden bird sailing off into the wind."

And Daniels added, "I think it made us all feel kind o' meek and prayerful like. It might have been a circus for some folks, but it wasn't any circus for us who had lived close by those Wright boys during all the months until we were as much wrapped up in the fate of the things as they were."

From Orville's diary, December 18: "Commence tearing down machine ready for packing."

From Bishop Milton Wright's diary, December 22: "I was at home all day. Reporters were calling and asking for pictures of the machine and of the boys."

From a letter to a newspaper: "My sons Wilbur and Orville are expected under the parental roof—always their home—within a few days. Wilbur is 36, Orville 32, and they are as inseparable as twins. For several years they have read up on aeronautics as a physician would read his books, and they have studied, discussed, and experimented together. Natural workmen, they have invented, constructed, and operated their gliders, and finally their 'Wright Flyer,' jointly, all at their own personal expense. About equal credit is due each."

And the bishop's entry on Christmas Day: "We as a family dine at Lorin's."

Ninety-nine years later, wanting to learn more about the haunting photograph of the Wrights' first flight, I drive to a suburb of Dayton. A veteran aviation photographer takes me down to his basement darkroom, closes the door, switches on an amber safelight. I can see him smile as he adjusts the enlarger lens. Dan Patterson started young, shooting sports for newspapers. He loved the nights spent developing film and making prints.

"I used to listen to the Rolling Stones in the dark, and dance around waiting for the images. There's magic in rooms like this; you never know what's going to come up."

I had met Dan at Dayton's Carillon Park. He was taking some new pictures of the 1905 Wright Flyer, on display there since 1950. It's the actual plane from the triumphant season at Huffman Prairie, restored under Orville Wright's direction. Dan has photographed it before; now the National Park Service had requested a shot with Orville's head on the brown-suited mannequin-pilot instead of Wilbur's.

"You want to see how it looks?" Dan asked that morning, inviting me to step on his stool and duck under the blackout cloth to see what was about to be recorded on Kodak Ektachrome in his four-by-five Wista field camera with a Schneider 150mm lens. He'd set up lights behind the plane so the background would disappear.

"Turn the focusing knob there on your right. Look right at the ground glass, don't try to see through the lens."

I could see an upside-down section of the wing. There was a luminous quality to the white fabric.

Dan said, "I love the translucence of the old wings. In World War I they started painting the planes and they lost that glowing light. The French had a camouflage paint. The brown had copper flecks in it, and the green had flecks of something else so it was iridescent on a plane. In the sun it would look one way and then differently in a cloud. The U.S. Air Force is spending millions trying to make their airplanes change color, and the French did it in 1915."

Now in his darkroom Dan is granting a favor I'd asked at Carillon Park. I wanted to see the first flight photograph take shape on paper, under the wash of developing solution.

"Sure," he'd said. "Come by tomorrow afternoon. I've got a terrific copy negative of that picture, and I love to print it."

Twenty years ago Dan was asked to copy a series of photographs for the archives at Wright State University. The glass plate negatives were long ago sent to the Library of Congress, but since many of them had been damaged in the 1913 Dayton flood, the prints in Wright State's collection, made before the flood, were often the best possible examples of the original photographs. Dan made copy negatives—of about twenty-five prints—with the understanding he'd keep a set for himself.

"I shot them in my studio, put them up at eye level with magnetized strips on a copy board that's fastened to the wall. I like to use four lights, bouncing off umbrella reflectors so it's indirect and real soft. You put the view camera on a tripod, and what I did was find the center of the photograph and run a piece of string out to the lens to make sure it's centered. Focus in with the bellows and you've got it."

Dan's making a contact print for me, employing the same method the Wrights often used. No enlarger is necessary. You put the negative in a holder, and project light down through it to the photo paper; in the old days you would simply lay the negative directly on the paper.

A fluorescent light flashes. A timer starts ticking. After twenty-three seconds, a beep. A sheet of Kodak paper now carries the image of the plane in the air. Using wooden tongs, Dan lifts the nascent print into a developing tray. Turns it over. After half a minute I start to see Wilbur's dark figure to the right, then the clean white edge lines of the lifting wings.

Dan says, "This would have been when Orville screamed out the darkroom door, 'Hey, we got it.'" The first clue would have come when they developed the negative and found they'd gotten home with a real picture. In a 1901 speech, Wilbur described what it had been like, working with the pictures of their first gliding experiments:

"In the photographic darkroom at home we pass moments of as thrilling interest as any in the field, when the image begins to appear on the plate and it is yet an open question whether we have a picture of a flying machine, or merely a patch of open sky."

Dan pins the print on a line to dry, and we go upstairs to his office, where he keeps a much larger first-flight photo on the wall. He says, "I've made huge enlargements of sections of this picture to study it. You dunk and splash around with the chemicals and ruin your shirts, but it's worth it to get the detail. Old photographs have a lot of spots, but if you really look at some of these things here in the sky—they're not just black specks— they're birds!"

In a decent print of this picture, a tiny bit of Wilbur's collar is visible, just a flash of white above his left shoulder. His suit coat is open in the wind, cap set tight. The profile of his face is visible against the faint gray of the beach and ocean, but you would know it's Wilbur anyway—he carries himself with more energy than Orville, and here his arms and legs seem caught in astonished motion.

Not that Orville seems relaxed, lying headfirst on the lower wing, trying to control this plane. His feet point at a stiff angle, and you can imagine how tense his toes must have been inside those shoes.

"Look at the wings," Dan says. "Sitting on the ground, this plane's wings have a pretty good droop to them, but here, you can see, when it developed lift and everything tightened the wings have come up and you think, wow, you know it's flying.

"And"—he points—"look at the footprints. This is the tension in the photograph. All these footprints all around but only one set comes out of this group and that's Wilbur, running along with the wing. Somewhere in these footprints are Orville's, and they would have stopped where he climbed on the plane. Then you have all the prints in a rectangle around that sawhorse where the lower right wing was resting, and you even see the wing's outline where those lifesaving guys who were helping couldn't walk. Most photographs record only a moment in time, but this one, to me, shows both things that happened that day. Those footprints, there, are from the era before they flew, and here, where the shutter clicks, this is flying. The world has changed. And it's the perfect photograph of that event."

The glass negative of the first-flight photograph stayed with Orville Wright until he died. It pleased him to be able to send out signed copies. Once he mailed a print to a teenager who sold him a program at an Ohio State football game in Columbus: the young man had returned an extra dollar bill that Orville had given him by mistake.

Many of the original prints were full-frame and carried Orville's signature in the lower left-hand corner. But that whole corner of the glass plate has been missing since the tumultuous Dayton flood—the water rose into the shed behind the family's Hawthorn Street home. Orville's later prints were cropped—reduced on all four sides so the chipped part wouldn't show.

The thin piece of glass, the negative for what is possibly the world's most-reproduced photograph, is now held secure within the files of the Prints and Photographs Division of the Library of Congress, in Washington, D.C. The label on the box says: LC-N86 DO NOT USE.

I'd made a formal request to see the first-flight glass negative, FedEx'd my credentials, appeared five minutes before my appointed Thursday afternoon time, stored my coat, briefcase, and pens in a researcher's locker. At precisely three-thirty Beverly Brannan appeared amid the long tables and rows of bookshelves, pushing a metal library cart, and smiling.

"Your timing is good," she says, opening the gate in the waist-high security enclosure. "We're starting a huge renovation here, and this plate's going to be unavailable. Everything around here will be a mess, I'm afraid."

We sit side by side at table number 6. From the top shelf of the cart she takes a blue fabric-covered pad, "a book cradle," she tells me, and the black box containing the negative. She is wearing white cotton gloves. I am not, having promised not even to breathe on the glass plate.

The box is heavy black cardboard. In addition to the library's file number, there's the familiar red-and-white warning sticker: GLASS—HANDLE WITH EXTREME CARE.

Beverly opens the box and slides out the acid-free manila sleeve that holds the negative folder. "We're having a new housing built for this negative. You can see it sort of rattles around in the box there. This is actually an old daguerreotype box, and those are smaller plates."

Then the actual piece of glass. She lays it lightly on the worn felt of the book cradle. This could be shattered, I think, lost forever. A light fixture could fall, or a ceiling panel. I look around the room—one of these people could throw a book over here!

"We don't know how this got broken, or when," Beverly says.

I offer the hypothesis that the corner's been missing since the 1913 flood. "People seem to think that piece of glass wound up in the mud on the floor of the Wrights' shed out back, where their darkroom was."

She laughs. "Well, the collective sense here would be that it's a great relief to know that we didn't do it."

With a tape measure, she checks the dimensions. Five-by-seven indeed. The glass—dark gray—looks to be delicate, brittle.

In addition to the corner damage, there are several sparkles where the edges have suffered tiny chips. LC-N86 was used to make prints, routinely, for decades, and a century has degraded the original image, as well as frigid winters and hot, humid summers. Now the negative is held in a 70-degree, 30-percent humidity room, and if you want a first-flight print, it's made from a copy negative or a digital scan.

"If you tilt this glass just right," she says, angling both the plate and her head, "and look at it just so . . . you can read the image as positive, and see the picture. It works that way against a dark background such as this photo box."

And, squinting a bit, I could see it. Wilbur in midstride, in ghostly negative on the glass surface, changes to black. The airplane wings are almost pure white.

"See this damage here, above the plane, these curving scratches in the emulsion? Someone's done that on purpose, probably trying to add more of a cloud effect. Photographers did a lot of that with the glass plates."

I ask Beverly if she thinks this really is the most reproduced photograph of all time, anywhere.

"How would you go about proving that?" she says. "I think there are two others that could make that claim. There's *Cimarron County, Oklahoma*—that's Arthur Renstrom's 1936 picture of a farmer and his son walking in the blowing dust. And of course, Dorothea Lange's *Migrant Mother*, although you'll see several versions of that picture. It's hard to say. You know we have two million images stored here."

If the Wrights had not thrilled America and Europe in 1908 and 1909, had not signed their military contracts and won their patent suits—the piece of glass that is now LC-N86 might have been mislaid, forgotten, or broken entirely. Photographers often scraped off the emulsion—the chemical coating that holds the image—and reused the glass negatives. Photographic plates sometimes became simple windowpanes; it's said that Mathew Brady images from the Civil War could once be found glazed into wooden frames in old greenhouses and barns.

It's a short walk down Capitol Hill from the Library of Congress to the Smithsonian's National Air and Space Museum. I want to go see the airplane itself—the Wright Flyer. It, too, might have been abandoned, aged into a dusty jumble of decaying wood and shredding fabric. But here it soars, the first plane you see when you pass through the museum's tall front doors.

It's not that high above you; it looks as if a basketball player could jump and touch the bottom of the skids. It is forty feet four inches wide, white cloth and bent sweeps of wood. The wings catch the light and reveal the spruce spars sewn inside the fabric. A model figure of Orville is prone in the pilot's position, looking straight ahead toward the National Mall. He is dressed, properly, in business suit and collar and tie, and cap. There's a worn spot on the upturned sole of his left shoe.

This machine, much of which is original to the first flight in 1903, was valued in 1948 by a Dayton probate court at one dollar. The appraisal was made shortly after Orville's death. And the *Dayton Daily News* carried this item, under the small headline:

INTANGIBLE

Judge Rodney Love of Probate court did the only thing a sensible man could do in admitting the first airplane of the Wright brothers for appraisal as part of the late Orville Wright's estate. He accepted a value of $1 which appraisers had put on the plane.

How could a man set a value—other than a token value—on the invention that brought to the world a tool ranking with the printing press, the wheel, and the fire with which savage man first learned to cook his food and warm his caves? The value of the Wright plane transcends the symbols of mathematics, and makes profanely out of order the measures of the market place.

The value of this plane approaches infinity. The only question—the burning question on which the future of civilization hangs—is whether man in his wisdom will put a plus sign before the infinitude, or whether in his folly he will place a minus sign that will plunge humanity into doom.

The 1903 Flyer was returned to the United States from London in 1948. During the war years the Science Museum there had stored the plane underground in a stone quarry tunnel, outside of London, to keep it safe from the Luftwaffe bombing raids. Orville's long feud with the Smithsonian ended in 1942, after mistakes were acknowledged and it was made clear that the Kitty Hawk machine represented the invention of the airplane.

Behind the 1903 plane, and higher, to the right, hangs Charles Lindbergh's *Spirit of St. Louis* (Lindbergh agreed to have his plane moved from its preeminent position when the Flyer arrived from London). The sound-barrier-breaking, burnt-orange Bell X-1 rocket plane is suspended nearby, named *Glamorous Glennis,* for

Chuck Yeager's wife. And at floor level, the capsules from John Glenn's first-orbit mission and Edward White's spacewalk.

Many visitors pause to look up at the Flyer. "Do you know why the wings are curved?" a young father asks his son, who nods uncertainly. A mother says, "It might be a replica of what their plane looked like then." Her little boy says, "They probably shined it."

For some time I stand near the display panel below the plane and listen as parents read the inscription to their children. In the words of Wilbur and Orville Wright:

THE FIRST FLIGHT LASTED ONLY TWELVE SECONDS, A FLIGHT VERY MODEST COMPARED WITH THAT OF BIRDS, BUT IT WAS NEVERTHELESS THE FIRST IN THE HISTORY OF THE WORLD IN WHICH A MACHINE CARRYING A MAN HAD RAISED ITSELF BY ITS OWN POWER INTO THE AIR IN FREE FLIGHT, HAD SAILED FORWARD ON A LEVEL COURSE WITHOUT REDUCTION OF SPEED, AND HAD FINALLY LANDED WITHOUT BEING WRECKED. THE SECOND AND THIRD FLIGHTS WERE A LITTLE LONGER, AND THE FOURTH LASTED 59 SECONDS COVERING A DISTANCE OF 852 FEET OVER THE GROUND AGAINST A 20 MILE WIND.

The sentences are etched into black marble, and ring with precision and cautious pride. The words describe both intention and accomplishment, and ask for no further recognition. As I look up at the handsome, handmade aircraft, I can see the clouds high above the windowed ceiling, drifting from west to east across a sky of afternoon light. Now there can be an airplane, a spacecraft, in that scene. Wilbur and Orville Wright, focused, willing to fail, finding physical pleasure in the work itself and joy in the sensation of flight, created a machine that moved with purpose through the element of air. Perhaps we've lost the ability to comprehend how that once seemed impossible, but we have the story of two brothers to assure us that someday, even in a century to come, such a thing might happen again.

AUTHOR'S NOTE

I HAVE A STACK OF BOOKS ON MY WRITING DESK, VALUED, trusted pages marked by scraps of paper—books without which my own would not be possible. Among them: *The Bishop's Boys,* by Tom Crouch; the prior biographies by Fred Howard and Fred Kelly; Peter Jakab's technical guide, *Visions of a Flying Machine;* Fred E. C. Culick and Spencer Dunmore's comprehensive *On Great White Wings.*

David Stick's book about the Outer Banks of North Carolina was essential, and I treasure our afternoon's conversation at his home on Kitty Hawk Bay. Also quite instructive and fun was a walk through Nags Head Woods with Jeff and Jan DeBlieu and their dog Cayenne, to see the freshwater "windowpane" ponds and the ever-moving dune called Run Hill.

At Manteo, North Carolina, my guides into the files of the Outer Banks History Center were KaeLi Spears, Sara Downing, and Brian Edwards. Bill Harris of Kitty Hawk helped with access to his oral history collection, which is housed there. And thanks to Ed Merrell and Wayne Matthews at the Museum of the Albemarle, in Elizabeth City, North Carolina.

In New York, at Columbia University's Butler Library, Mary Marshall Clark welcomed me to the Oral History Research Office and found interviews with aviation pioneers, including the air show promoter Ross Browne.

I was always happy to find a need to visit Catharine Allen and her staff and volunteers at the College Park Aviation Museum in Maryland.

Len Bruno of the Library of Congress provided archival expertise and patient encouragement. Peter Jakab of the National Air and Space Museum explained matters of lift and drag. Also thanks to NPR's David Kestenbaum.

At Wright State University's Special Collections at Paul Laurence Dunbar Library, Dawne Dewey, John Sanford, Jane Wildermuth, and John Armstrong became almost colleagues during my summer's stay in the Dayton area. Also helpful were Claudia Watson, Curt Dalton, and Jeff Opt of the Montgomery County Historical Society, Nancy Horlacher and Mary Kay Mabe of Carillon Park, Leon Bey of the Dayton and Montgomery County Library, and Marjorie McLellan of Wright State. Any historical missteps though, will be mine, not theirs.

A neighbor's recollection of Orville at Hawthorn Hill is from the Wright Brothers Oral History Tapes, University of Dayton Archives.

Thanks to Betty Darst of Dayton, who performs a living biography of Katharine Wright, for sharing her experience and knowledge.

It was Dawne Dewey who first mentioned Katharine's correspondence with Henry Haskell, available on microfilm at Wright State. And then playwright Tony Dallas, in a chance encounter one evening in nearby Yellow Springs, said, "Be sure you look at Katharine's letters."

Henry Haskell's letter to his friend (Griffith Brewer) in London, excerpted in the Hawthorn Hill chapter, is from the Collection of the Royal Aeronautical Society, London.

I learned of Jacques Henri Lartigue's Wilbur Wright photograph in Adam Gopnik's book, *Paris to the Moon*. Melissa Block translated the comments of the young Lartigue. The Marguerite Yourcenar epigraph was inspired by its use as such in *Jacques Henri Lartigue, Photographer*.

For other help with photographs I thank Jeffrey John and Ron Geibert of Wright State; Jerome Ennels of Maxwell Air Force Base, in Alabama; Darrel Collins of the National Park Service, Kill Devil Hills; and Alex Nyerges of the Dayton Art Institute. And Neenah Ellis, who served as photo editor as well as general researcher.

Chris Kidder of Manteo, North Carolina, and Mark Bernstein of Yellow Springs, both writers, read early drafts of these pages, returning helpful notes.

Paul Glenshaw of Silver Spring, Maryland, has been an advisor almost from the beginning. He's the website designer for wrightexperience.com. (Another useful site is Nick Engler's first-to-fly.com.)

At Crown Publishers, Steve Ross always has a smile in his voice when I call. This is our second book together, and I treasure his willingness to let me take off with no clear destination and a vague arrival time. My editor is Annik Lafarge. Her guidance has made every page better and she's been a delight to work with. Thanks, again, to my agents, Jonathon Lazear and Christi Cardenas.

Every author knows this final paragraph of an acknowledgements section often has a much deeper subtext. A few words must stand for many. I thank my wife Neenah. I cannot imagine writing a book without the support of her love and her talent. My spirits fly when I think of her.

BIBLIOGRAPHY

d'Astier, Martine, and Pierre Borhan. *Les Envols de Jacques Henri Lartigue.* Paris: Edition Phillipe Sers/Association des Amis de Jacques Henri Lartigue, 1989.

Bernstein, Mark. *Grand Eccentrics: Turning the Century: Dayton and the Inventing of America.* Wilmington, Ohio: Orange Frazer Press, 1996.

————. *Gentleman Amateurs: An Appreciation of Wilbur and Orville Wright.* Dayton, Ohio: *Dayton Daily News,* 2002.

Caidin, Martin. *Barnstorming.* 1965. Reprint: New York: Bantam Books, 1991.

Combs, Harry, with Martin Caiden. *Kill Devil Hill: Discovering the Secret of the Wright Brothers.* Boston: Houghton Mifflin Company, 1979.

Crouch, Tom D. *The Bishop's Boys: A Life of Wilbur and Orville Wright.* New York: W. W. Norton & Company, 1990.

Culick, Fred E. C., and Spencer Dunmore. *On Great White Wings.* New York: Hyperion/Madison Press, 2001.

Dalton, Curt. *The Terrible Resurrection.* Dayton, Ohio: 2002.

DeBlieu, Jan. *Wind: How the Flow of Air Has Shaped Life, Myth, and the Land.* Boston: Houghton Mifflin Company, 1998.

Deines, Ann, ed. *Wilbur and Orville Wright: A Handbook of Facts.* Eastern National, 2001.

DuFour, H. R., and Peter J. Unitt. *Charles E. Taylor: The Wright Brothers Mechanician*. Dayton, Ohio: Prime Printing, 1997.

Fisk, Fred C., and Marlin W. Todd. *The Wright Brothers from Bicycle to Biplane: An Illustrated History of the Wright Brothers*. Dayton, Ohio: 2000.

Freedman, Russell. *The Wright Brothers: How They Invented the Airplane*. New York: Holiday House, 1991.

Geibert, Ronald R., and Tucker Malishenko, eds. *Early Flight: 1900–1911 Original Photographs from the Wright Brothers Personal Collection*. Dayton, Ohio: Landfall Press, 1984.

————, and Patrick B. Nolan. *Kitty Hawk and Beyond: The Wright Brothers and the Early Years of Aviation*. Lanham, Maryland: Roberts Rinehart Publishers, 2003.

Gibbs-Smith, C. H. *The Wright Brothers: Aviation Pioneers and Their Work 1899–1911*. 1963. Reprint: London: NMSI Trading Ltd, 2002.

Glines, Colonel C. V., USAF. *From the Wright Brothers to the Astronauts: The Memoirs of Major General Benjamin D. Foulois*. New York: McGraw-Hill Book Company, 1968.

Hairr, John. *Images of America: Outer Banks*. Charleston, South Carolina: Arcadia Publishing, 2001.

Hamblyn, Richard. *The Invention of Clouds: How an Amateur Meteorologist Forged the Language of the Skies*. New York: Farrar, Straus, and Giroux, 2001.

Howard, Fred. *Wilbur and Orville: A Biography of the Wright Brothers*. 1988. Reprint: Mineola, New York: Dover Publications, Inc., 1998.

Jakab, Peter L. *Visions of a Flying Machine: The Wright Brothers and the Process of Invention*. Washington, D.C.: Smithsonian Institution Press, 1990.

————, and Rick Young, eds. *The Published Writings of Wilbur and Orville Wright*. Washington, D.C.: Smithsonian Institution Press, 2000.

Johnson, Mary Ann. *A Field Guide to Flight: On the Aviation Trail in Dayton, Ohio*. Dayton, Ohio: Landfall Press, 1996.

Kelly, Fred C. *The Wright Brothers: A Biography*. 1943. Reprint: Mineola, New York: Dover Publications, Inc., 1989.

————, ed. *Miracle at Kitty Hawk: The Letters of Wilbur and Orville Wright*. 1951. Reprint: New York: Da Capo Press, 1996.

Kidder, Chris. *Aloft at Last: How the Wright Brothers Made History*. Nags Head, North Carolina: Nags Head Arts, Inc., 2002.

Kirk, Stephen. *First in Flight: The Wright Brothers in North Carolina*. Winston-Salem, North Carolina: John F. Blair Publisher, 1995.

Lande, D. A. *Oshkosh—Gateway to Aviation: 50 Years of EAA Fly-Ins*. Oshkosh, Wisconsin: Experimental Aircraft Association, 2002.

Lewis, Cecil. *Sagittarius Rising.* Harrisburg, Pennsylvania: Stackpole Books, 1963.

McFarland, Marvin W., ed. *The Papers of Wilbur and Orville Wright: Including the Chanute-Wright Letters,* 2 vols. 1953. Reprint: New York: McGraw-Hill, 2001.

McKee, Alexander. *The Friendless Sky: The Story of Air Combat in World War I.* New York: William Morrow and Company, 1964.

McKee, Phillip. *Big Town.* New York: John Day, 1931.

Mobley, Joe A. *Ship Ashore: The U.S. Lifesavers of Coastal North Carolina.* Raleigh, North Carolina: Division of Archives and History, North Carolina Department of Cultural Resources, 1994.

Parramore, Thomas C. *Triumph at Kitty Hawk: The Wright Brothers and Powered Flight.* Raleigh, North Carolina: Division of Archives and History, North Carolina Department of Cultural Resources, 1993.

————. *First to Fly: North Carolina and the Beginnings of Aviation.* Chapel Hill, North Carolina: The University of North Carolina Press, 2002.

Renstrom, Arthur G., comp. *Wilbur and Orville Wright: A Bibliography.* Washington, D.C.: Library of Congress, 1968.

————. *Wilbur & Orville Wright: A Chronology.* Washington, D.C.: Library of Congress, 1975.

————. *Wilbur and Orville Wright: Pictorial Materials,* Washington, D.C.: Library of Congress, 1982.

Rountree, Susan Byrum. *Nags Headers.* Winston-Salem, North Carolina: John F. Blair, 2001.

Rollins, Ron, ed. *For the Love of Dayton: Life in the Miami Valley 1796–2001.* Dayton, Ohio: *Dayton Daily News,* 2001.

Sharp, Archibald. *Bicycles and Tricycles: An Elementary Treatise on Their Design and Construction.* 1896. Reprint: Cambridge, Massachusetts: MIT Press, 1977.

Stick, David. *The Outer Banks of North Carolina 1584–1958,* Chapel Hill, North Carolina: The University of North Carolina Press, 1958.

Stoff, Joshua. *Picture History of Aviation.* Mineola, New York: Dover Publications, 1996.

Szurovy, Geza, and Mike Goulian. *Basic Aerobatics.* New York: TAB Books, 1994.

Wagstaff, Patty, with Ann L. Cooper. *Fire and Air: A Life on the Edge.* Chicago: Chicago Review Press, Inc., 1997.

Winters, Nancy. *Man Flies: The Story of Alberto Santos-Dumont, Master of the Balloon.* Great Britain: Bloomsbury, 1997.

Wright, David, and David Zoby. *Fire on the Beach: Recovering the Lost Story of Richard Etheridge and the Pea Island Lifesavers.* New York: Scribner, 2000.

Wright, Milton. *Diaries: 1857–1917.* Dayton, Ohio: Wright State University, 1999.

Wright, Orville. *How We Invented the Airplane: An Illustrated History.* 1953. Reprint: Mineola, New York: Dover Publications, 1988.

Yeager, Gen. Chuck, and Leo Janos. *Yeager: An Autobiography.* New York: Bantam Books, 1985.

Collections

The Columbia University Oral History Collection, The Rare Book and Manuscript Library, Butler Library, Columbia University, New York, New York.

Katharine Wright Haskell and Henry Haskell Letters to Griffith Brewer: The Collection of the Royal Aeronautical Society, London, England.

Katharine Wright Haskell Papers: The Western Historical Manuscript Collection at Kansas City, a joint collection of the University of Missouri and the State Historical Society of Missouri.

The Papers of Wilbur and Orville Wright: Manuscript Division, Library of Congress, Washington, D.C.

Wright Brothers/Charles F. Kettering Oral History Project Archives Collection, Albert Emanuel Hall, University of Dayton, Dayton, Ohio.

Wright Brothers Negatives: Prints and Photographs Division, Library of Congress, Washington, D.C.

Wright Brothers: Special Collections and Archives, Wright State University Libraries, Dayton, Ohio.

CREDITS

Five Portraits

Susan Catherine Koerner Wright, Bishop Milton Wright, Katharine Wright, Wilbur Wright, Orville Wright. There exists no complete family photograph of the Wrights, not even of the bishop and his three younger children all together.

Courtesy of Special Collections and Archives, Wright State University.

Statue of Liberty

Wilbur Wright leaves Governors Island in New York Harbor during the Hudson-Fulton celebration on September 30, 1909, with the Statue of Liberty in the distance. A reporter observed: "As he swept out over the harbor he came between the sinking sun and the crowd. The plane was turned to a delicate pink."

Photo by: Unknown. Courtesy of Special Collections and Archives, Wright State University.

Woodland Cemetery

Wilbur Wright's funeral procession climbs the hill toward the family gravesite in Dayton's Woodland Cemetery on June 1, 1912.

Photo by: William Mayfield. The Marvin Christian Collection.

To Kitty Hawk

The surfmen of the Kitty Hawk Life-Saving Station, taken during Orville and Wilbur's first visit in 1900. The Wrights arrived knowing no one, but made many friends by the time of the powered flight. *Left to right:* Robert Lee Griggs, Robert Fulton Sanderlin, Thomas E. "Tom Ed" Hines, Joseph Edward "Joe Ed" Baum (cook), keeper Samuel J. Payne, James Riley Best, and Thomas Nelson Sanderlin. The dog's name is lost to history.

Photo by: Wright Brothers. Library of Congress, Prints and Photographs Division [LC-DIG-ppprs-00551].

Pilots and Planes

One of the brothers flying a 1902 glider off Big Kill Devil Hill. Their camp is visible below, the Atlantic Ocean on the horizon.

Photo by: Wright Brothers. Courtesy of Special Collections and Archives, Wright State University.

Huffman Prairie

Orville in the 85th flight of the Wright 1904 Flyer at Huffman Prairie, east of Dayton, the modern-day site of Wright-Patterson Air Force Base. Wednesday, November 16, 1904.

Photo by: Wright Brothers. Library of Congress, Prints and Photographs Division [LC-DIG-ppprs-00616].

Above France

Wilbur Wright et sa fameuse casquette: An exhausted Wilbur "and his famous cap," which caused a sensation in France. Photo taken by the child prodigy photographer Jacques Henri Lartigue, age 15. February, 1909, Pau, France.

Photograph by Jacques Henri Lartigue © Ministère de la Culture–France/AAJHL.

CREDITS

Fort Myer

Spectators try to extricate the gravely injured Army Lieutenant Thomas Selfridge from the wreckage of the Wright Flyer as Orville lies unconscious on the ground to the right. September 17, 1908, just outside the western wall of Arlington Cemetery.

Photo by: C. H. Claudy. Courtesy of Special Collections and Archives, Wright State University.

New York Harbor

Wilbur meticulously prepares for his flight up the Hudson River with a newly purchased canoe strapped to the skids of the Wright Flyer as an emergency flotation device. October 4, 1909.

Photo by: Paul Thompson. Courtesy Special Collections and Archives, Wright State University.

The Oshkosh Air Show

Orville in his flying goggles with student pilots in Montgomery, Alabama, in the spring of 1910. Within two years, both Hoxsey and Welsh were killed in flying exhibitions. Neither Crane nor Davis qualified as pilots.

Left to right: Arthur L. Welsh, Spencer Crane, Orville Wright, Walter Brookins, James Davis, and Archibald Hoxsey.

Photo by: Unknown. Courtesy of Special Collections and Archives, Wright State University.

Hawthorn Hill

Orville, Katharine, and Bishop Milton Wright moved here after Wilbur's death. Orville's bedroom is at the far left on the second floor with the window open. Katharine's is in the center, behind the small balcony. From the privacy of her desk there she wrote hundreds of letters to her future husband, Henry Haskell.

Photo by: Orville Wright. Library of Congress, Prints and Photographs Division [LC-DIG-ppprs-00742].

CREDITS

First Flight

The first flight photograph, from the Wrights' original glass plate negative, damaged in the Dayton flood of 1913, now housed at the Library of Congress in Washington, D.C.

Photo by: John T. Daniels, surfman from the Kill Devil Hills Lifesaving Station. Library of Congress, Prints and Photographs Division [LC-DIG-ppprs-00626].

INDEX

Aerial Experiment Association, 103–104
Aerobatics, 143–145
Aero-Club de France, 79
Aerodrome Number 5, 14, 168
Aeronautical competition, 65
Air density, 50, 65
Airfoil design, 51
"Air Voyage up the Hudson, The"
    (McKaye), 130–131
Albany, New York, 123
Albemarle Sound, North Carolina, 21, 24,
    30, 31, 36, 185, 186
Alexander, Jim, 47
Alfonso, King of Spain, 109
American Wright Company, Dayton, Ohio,
    146–147
Arlington National Cemetery, 95, 102, 104,
    108, 113

B-2 Spirit Stealth bomber, 184–185
Balloons, 79–81, 96
Basic Aerobatics, 143
Baum, Elijah, 33, 35
Beachey, Lincoln, 148
Beck, Agnes, 174

Bedloe's Island, New York, 128
Bell, Alexander Graham, 100, 101, 103
Bell X-1 rocket plane, 16, 200
Belmont Park, New York, 149, 152
Berlin, Germany, 118
Bernier, Steve, 43–45
Big Hill, Kitty Hawk, 189, 191
Blériot, Louis, 83, 84, 118
Boeing 747, 77
Boeing 777, 77
Bollée, Léon, 88
Bombeck, Erma, 7
Brady, Mathew, 199
Brannan, Beverly, 196–197
Brookins, Walter, 147–148, 152
Brooklyn Bridge, New York, 122, 124
Browne, Ross, 153–154
Bush, George W., 121
Buttermilk Channel, New York, 123, 127

Cannon, Burrell, 66
Cayley, Sir George, 13
Centocelle, Italy, 110
Cernan, Gene, 139
Challice, Scott, 185–186

I N D E X

Chanute, Octave, 26, 44, 51, 65, 111
Charles, Jacques, 80
Charles Flint & Company, 82
Chesapeake & Ohio Railroad, xii, 22
Chicago World's Fair (1893), 22
Cimarron County, Oklahoma (Renstrom), 198
Civil War, 96, 199
Clark, Robert, 101
Clay, Henry, 99
Clermont (paddlewheel), 123, 124
Clouds, 73–74
College Park, Maryland, 132
Collington Island, North Carolina, 32
Combs, Harry, 65
Concorde, 77
Cosmos Club, Washington, D.C., 99, 111
Cox, James, 10
Cubana Airlines, 140
Curlicue (fishing schooner), 23, 28, 29, 31–33
Currituck Sound, North Carolina, 24
Curtiss, Glenn Hammond, 103, 104, 118, 124–127, 129, 148, 168
Cygnet (kite), 103–104

Daniels, John T., 190, 191
Dayton, Ohio, 3–9, 14, 16, 17, 111
    flood of 1913, 54, 193, 196, 197
    Huffman Prairie Flying Field, 15, 62–74, 79, 98, 102, 147, 192
    Woodland Cemetery, 3–9, 14, 16, 17, 160
    Wright brothers homecoming celebrations (1909), 111–112
Dayton, Springfield & Urbana Interurban Railway, 63
Dayton Daily News, 10, 63, 199–200
Dayton Evening Herald, 10, 63
Delagrange, Léon, 91
Diaries: 1857–1917 (Bishop Wright), 11–13, 15, 95, 104, 109, 111, 159–161, 191–192
Dosher, J. J., 26
Drag, 50
Drake (warship), 130

Dunbar, Matilda, 6
Dunbar, Paul Laurence, 6

Earhart, Amelia, 34
East River, New York, 122, 123
Edward VII, King of England, 110
Eiffel Tower, Paris, 78–79, 83
Elizabeth City, North Carolina, 21, 27–29, 186, 187
Emergency flotation device, 122
Engler, Nick, 47
English Channel, 92
Exhibition flying, 146–152
Experimental Aircraft Association (EAA), 138–141
Extra, Walter, 144
Ezekiel Airship Company, Texas, 66

F-14 Tomcat, 185
Farnam, Henri, 83
Federal Aviation Administration (FAA), 138, 140, 141
Fire and Air: A Life on the Edge (Wagstaff), 143
First flight, twentieth anniversary of, 165
Flyer (dog), 84
Flying Circus tour, 153
Flying safety, Orville Wright on, 146–147
Fort Jay, Governors Island, 121
Fort Myer, Virginia, 89, 92, 95–108, 111–114
Foulois, Benjamin, 112–114
France, 51, 70, 78–92, 102, 107, 109–110, 118, 124, 193
Friedrich Wilhelm, Prince, 119
Fulton, Robert, 123–125
Furnas, Charles, 98

Garros, Roland, 83, 152, 153
Gemini space capsule, 56
General Services Administration, 120, 121
Georgian Bay, Lake Huron, 171–172, 175
Germany, 118, 119, 124
Glamorous Glennis (X-1 rocket plane), 200
Gleanings in Bee Culture (journal), 67
Glenn, John, 198
Glider flights (1900–1902), 26, 35–39, 45–46, 49–52

Goffigon, Cumpston, 23
Governors Island, New York, 117, 120–125,
    128, 131
Grande Semaine d'Aviation de la
    Champagne, 118, 119, 124
Grandfather Mountain, North Carolina, 44
Grant's Tomb, New York, 122, 124, 129,
    130, 132
Gray, Rose, 159, 178
Great Aerodrome, 14
Great Britain, 70, 118, 124, 167, 168
Great Miami River, 63
Grumbach, Carrie, 160, 176
Gulf Stream, 25

Hadden, Bill, 56
Half Moon (ship), 123, 124
Hamilton, Charles, 148
Hang gliding, 43–47
Harper's Weekly, 124, 146
Haskell, Henry J., 16, 163–167, 169–178
Haskell, Isabel, 163, 169
Haskell, Katharine Wright, 11, 21–22, 33,
    63, 118, 147, 149
    correspondence with brothers, 36–38,
        78, 82, 88, 89, 99, 106–108,
        119–120, 187–188
    correspondence with father, 35, 160
    death of, 16, 175
    education of, 15
    finances of, 172–173
    in France, 109–110
    grave of, 5, 16
    at Hawthorn Hill, 159, 162, 171
    marriage and courtship of, 16,
        162–167, 170–175
    Orville and, 16, 161, 169–175
    Orville's accident and, 106–107
    Smithsonian controversy and, 167
    as teacher, xiii, 163–164
    twentieth anniversary of first flight and,
        163
Hawthorn Hill, Oakwood, Ohio, 16,
    159–162, 171, 178, 179
H&D Folsom Arms Company, 122
Henry, John, 23
Holien, Kim, 96, 98, 100, 101, 103, 104

Howard, Luke, 73
Hoxsey, Arch, 147–149, 152
Hudec, Marianne Miller, 54
Hudson, Henry, 123–125
Hudson-Fulton Celebration, New York,
    117, 120, 122–132
Hudson River, New York, 117, 122, 124,
    129
Huffman, George, 10
Huffman, Torrence, 62, 64
Huffman Prairie Flying Field, Ohio, 15,
    62–74, 79, 98, 102, 147, 192
Hurricane Floyd, 32–33
Hyde, Ken, 51–54, 56

Indiana Dunes, Lake Michigan, 26
Indianapolis Motor Speedway, 148
International Aviation Tournament, New
    York (1910), 149, 152

Jackson, George, 28, 29
James, Wayne, 187
Jameson, John, 173
Jameson, Leontine, 173
Jockey's Ridge State Park, North Carolina,
    32, 43, 44, 46–47, 49, 186
John Doe (airplane), 142
Johnstone, Ralph, 147–152
June Bug (biplane), 104

Kansas City Star, 163, 170
Kettering, Charles, 10
Kill Devil Hill, North Carolina, 32, 34, 37,
    43, 52, 155, 183, 187, 189, 191
King, Henry Churchill, 175
Kitty Hawk (see Wright brothers)
Kitty Hawk Bay, North Carolina, 30, 32, 35
Kitty Hawk Kites, 43–45
Kitty Hawk Life-Saving Station, 188
Korona V camera, 188, 190

La Guardia, Fiorello, 122
Lahm, Frank, 102
Lake Huron, 170–172, 174
Lake Winnebago, 137
Lambert Island, Lake Huron, 171–172, 174
Landman, Drew, 55

Lange, Dorothea, 198
Langley, Samuel P., 14, 168, 170
Langley Air Force Base, Hampton, Virginia, 54, 55
Langley Full Scale Tunnel, 55
Lartigue, Jacques Henri, 84–85
Launch track system, 64
Lebrecque, Harry, 152–153
Le Figaro (newspaper), 91
Le Havre, France, 88
Le Mans, France, 84, 86–93, 98
Les Hunaudières, France, 90–91
Lewis, Cecil, 73–74
Library of Congress, 193, 196–199
Lift, 48–50
Lilienthal, Otto, 44, 50
Lindbergh, Charles, 83, 178–179, 200
London Daily Mail, 118
Louisiana Purchase of 1803, 65
Love, Rodney, 199
Lovell, James, 139
Lucas, Terri, 61–62, 70–71
Lusitania (liner), 128

Madison, Dolley, 99
Mad River, 62
Manhattan Island, New York, 117, 120–132
Manly, Charles, 14
Manteo, North Carolina, 187
Marconi, Guglielmo, 127–128
Markow, Tanya, 47, 48
Mason, Alexander, 125–127
McCrone laboratory, 54
McKaye, Percy, 130–131
Mechanix Illustrated, 138
Metzler, Eric, 71–72
Meyer, Dave, 54
Michelin Prize, 92, 110
Migrant Mother (Lange), 196
Miller, Polly, 96, 103
Ministry of War (France), 79, 82
Miscione, Renée, 120–122, 129
Moisant, Alfred, 153
Moisant, John, 149, 153
Montgomery, Alabama, 146–147
Morehouse, Johnny, 7–8
Musée de l'Air et de L'Espace, France, 83–84

Nags Head, North Carolina, 35
NASCAR racing teams, 55–56
National Aeronautics and Space Administration (NASA), 55
National Air and Space Museum, Washington, D.C., 83, 100, 101, 197
National Archives, 101
National Cash Register Company, 163
National Park Service, 34, 52, 121, 190
New Jersey Palisades, 117
New River, 22
New York American, 150
New York Herald, 125
Nicolaou, Stéphane, 84
Night flying, 119, 147–148
Nolin, Dave, 70
Norfolk & Southern Railroad, 21
Northcliffe, Lord, 118
Northeastern High School Orchestral Band, Elizabeth City, 186–187
North River, 31, 32
Nusbaum, Steve, 141–142

Oakwood, Ohio, 16, 159–162, 171, 177, 179
Oberlin College, xiii, 15, 161, 163, 170, 175–177
Ohman, Klaus, 47–49
Oshkosh, Wisconsin, 135–145, 154–155
Outer Banks, 21, 24–25, 27, 30, 35
Outer Banks History Center, 35

P-51 Mustangs, 140
Pamlico Sound, 24
Paris, France, 77, 78
Parks, Larry, 54
Pasquotank River, 21, 27–30, 33
Pataki, George, 121
Patent infringements, 10–11, 104, 137, 188
Patterson, Dan, 192–194
Patterson, Frank Stuart, 62
Patterson, John, 10
Pau, France, 84, 85, 109–110
Pégoud, Adolphe, 83–84
Pénaud, Alphonse, 13
Perry, Israel, 23, 28, 30, 31

I N D E X

Photographs, by Wright brothers, 188–190, 192–198

Pilot training, 110, 147–148

Pine Island, Florida, 26

Pittsburg, Texas, 66

Poberezny, Audrey, 138

Poberezny, Paul, 138

Potomac River, 14, 89, 95, 112, 166

Potsdam, Germany, 118, 119

Press coverage of Wright brothers, 63, 91, 99, 110–111, 118, 125–126

Pride of the West muslin, 54

Propellers, 53–54, 69

Radius, Manfred, 154

Reckendorf, Enno, 27–33

Red Barons, 143

Red Wing (biplane), 104

Reims, France, 118, 119, 124

Reims Racer (airplane), 118, 125

Renstrom, Arthur, 196

Replicas, 46–49, 52–57

Richter, Elizabeth, 9

Richthofen, Baron Manfred von, 141, 153

Rickenbacker, Eddie, 172

RMS *Campania*, 78

Roanoke Island, 22, 23, 184, 185, 187

Roanoke Sound, 24

Robert, Marie-Noel, 80

Rogallo, Francis, 44, 55

Rogallo, Gertrude, 44

Root, A. I., 67–68, 69

Rutan, Dick, 139

Sagittarius Rising (Lewis), 73

Sailplanes, 154

St. Louis World's Fair, 65, 66

Sandegren, Jim, 3–9, 14–15

Santos-Dumont, Alberto, 79, 83

Science Museum, London, 167, 168

Scientific American, 81

Seat belts, 119

Selfridge, Thomas, 92, 98, 103–106, 108–109

Selfridge Gate, Fort Myer, Virginia, 108

Shooter's Hill, Virginia, 112, 113

Shroud of Turin, 54

Simms Station, Ohio, 63, 65

Smeaton, John, 50

Smeaton's coefficient, 50

Smithsonian Institution, 13–14, 167–170
    National Air and Space Museum, 83, 100, 101, 199

Sousa, John Philip, 187

Spirit of St. Louis (airplane), 178, 200

Squier, George, 108

Stanley, King Levi, 9

Stanley, Owen, 9

Stanley, Queen Matilda, 9

Stardust Twins, 149

Statue of Liberty, New York, 117, 122, 127, 128

Stearman biplane, 143

Stick, David, 33–34

Stick, Frank, 34

Strategic Air Command (SAC), 62

Taft, William Howard, 101, 111

Takeoff acceleration, 66

Tate, Addie, 26, 33, 35–37

Tate, William J., 26–27, 33, 35–36

Taylor, Charlie, 50, 62, 66, 73, 98, 124, 131, 147, 189

Tri-Motor airplane, 139

Typhoid fever, 12, 36

United Brethren Church, xiii, 15, 160

United States Air Force, 17, 97, 193

United States Army, 14, 120
    Fort Myer, Virginia, 89, 92, 95–108, 111–114

United States Coast Guard, 120, 121

United States Custom House, New York, 129

United States Life-Saving Service, 25

United States Signal Corps, 96, 98, 113, 114

United States Weather Bureau, 26

U.S. Department of Defense, 47

U.S. Department of War, 70, 89, 112

Van Deman, Sarah, 132

Victoria, Queen of England, 6

Voisin, Charles, 83

Voyager (airplane), 139

Waco biplane, 185–186
Wade Point Light, 30–31
Wagner, Bob, 142–143
Wagner, Pat, 142–143
Wagstaff, Patty, 143–145
Walcott, Charles, 168
Warfare, Orville Wright on airplane use in, 114
Washington *Evening Star*, 132
Webbert, Charlie, 66–67
Webster, Daniel, 99
Weight-drop system, 66–67, 102
Wellman, Haskell, xii–xiii
Welsh, A. L., 147
Werthner, William, 160
Western Historical Manuscript Collection, Kansas City, 162
Western Society of Engineers, 50
Western Union, 82
White, Edward, 200
Whiteman Air Force Base, Missouri, 183
Wills Wing Condor, 44
Wind-tunnel experiments of, 50–51
Wing warping, theory of, 26, 104
Wisconsin State Fair, 149
Woodland Cemetery, Dayton, Ohio, 3–9, 14, 16, 17, 160
World War I, 114, 153, 193
World War II, 16, 86, 140
Wright, Bishop Milton, xiii, 5, 63
    correspondence with Katharine, 35, 162
    correspondence with Wilbur, 79–81, 90, 105–106
    death of, 161
    diary entries by, 11–13, 15, 95, 104, 109, 111, 159–161, 191–192
    at Hawthorn Hill, 158–159
    as missionary, 22
Wright, Ida, 5
Wright, Katharine (*see* Haskell, Katharine Wright)
Wright, Lorin, 5, 63, 106, 174–177, 188, 192
Wright, Netta, 175
Wright, Orville (*see also* Wright brothers):
    accident at Fort Myer, 92, 104–106
    on airplane use in warfare, 114

book project of, 164, 165
correspondence with Wilbur, 82, 88–90, 103
death of, 17, 177
on flying safety, 146–147
Fort Myer trials and, 95, 98–108, 112–114
in France, 109, 110
in Germany, 118, 119
at Hawthorn Hill, 159–162, 178–179
health of, 36, 164, 171, 174
later years of, 16
sister Katharine and, 16, 163, 171–175
Smithsonian controversy about 1903 Flyer, 167–169
writing and, 164
Wright, Otis, 5
Wright, Reuchlin, 5
Wright, Susan C., 5, 160, 162
Wright, Wilbur (*see also* Wright brothers):
    accident in France, 89
    on ballooning, 81
    correspondence with father, 79–81, 90, 105–106
    correspondence with Orville, 82, 88–90, 103
    death of, 10, 13, 36
    Fort Myer trials and, 112–113
    in France, 51, 78–82, 84–92, 102, 107, 109–110
    at Hawthorn Hill, 160
    health of, 12
    Hudson-Fulton Celebration, New York, 117, 120, 122, 124–132
    on Orville's accident, 105–106
    Smithsonian Institution, letters to, 13–14
    wing warping, theory of, 26, 104
    writing and, 164
Wright brothers:
    airplane business, 70, 78, 87–89, 97, 118
    bicycle business, xiii, 50, 63
    burial plot, 3–6, 17
    correspondence with sister, 36–38, 78, 82, 88, 89, 99, 106–108, 119–120, 187–188
    exhibition flying and, 146–152
    fame of, 110–111

family relations, 14–16

finances of, 117, 118

first flight instrument, 57

first published eyewitness account of flight (1904), 68

first trip to Kitty Hawk (1900), 26–39

glider flights (1900–1902), 26, 35–39, 45–46, 49–52

homecoming celebrations (1909), 111–112

at Huffman Prairie Flying Field, 62–70, 73, 74, 79, 102, 192

launch track system and, 64

memorial on Kitty Hawk, xii, 32, 34, 181–185

1903 flights, xi, xii, 62–64, 183–184, 187–196, 201

1904 flights, 63–68

1905 flights, 69–70, 192

only flight together, 15

patent infringements and, 10–11, 104, 137, 188

photographs by, 188–190, 192–198

pilot training and, 110, 147–148

pitch, roll, and yaw, 69

press coverage of, 63, 91, 99, 110–111, 118, 125–126

printing business, xiii, 6

propellers and, 53, 69

takeoff acceleration and, 66

turning of plane and, 68, 69

twentieth anniversary of first flight, 163

weight-drop system and, 66–67, 102

wind-tunnel experiments of, 50–51

Wright Brothers Aeroplane Company, 47

Wright Brothers National Memorial site, Kitty Hawk, xii, 32, 34

Wright Brothers National memorial site, Kitty Hawk, 183–187

Wright Experience team, 52–53, 56

Wright Field, Dayton, 16

Wright Gate, Fort Myer, Virginia, 108

Wright-Patterson Air Force Base, Ohio, 17, 61–62, 70–71, 73

Wright State University, 63, 97, 193

Wuichet, James, 8

X-1 rocket plane, 16, 200

Yeager, Chuck, 16, 139, 200–201

ABOUT THE AUTHOR

Noah Adams, the longtime host of *All Things Considered,* is a correspondent for National Public Radio. He is the author of *Piano Lessons, Far Appalachia, Saint Croix Notes,* and *Noah Adams and "All Things Considered": A Radio Journal.* He lives in the Washington, D.C., area with his wife, Neenah Ellis.